Kukulcan

Who is Quetzalcoatl?

By

Julia SvadiHatra

Kukulcan

Kukulcan
Who is Quetzalcoatl?
Copyright © 2009 by Julia SvadiHatra

iUniverse books may be ordered through booksellers or by contacting:

iUniverse
1663 Liberty Drive
Bloomington, IN 47403
www.iuniverse.com
1-800-Authors (1-800-288-4677)

ISBN: 978-1-4401-4104-1 (pbk)
ISBN: 978-1-4401-4105-8 (ebk)

Printed in the United States of America

Editor: Roxane Christ - www.1steditor.biz

Cover design Most4u.net

Thank you for the Deep Dive Spiral image on the cover to:
http://www.sgeier.net/fractals/indexe.php
The Creator
The fractals here were created by Sven Geier, who is currently employed by the Jet Propulsion Laboratory (JPL); a division of the California Institute of Technology and a center of the National Aeronautics and Space Administration (NASA).

Dedication

Dedicated to the creativity of the people who lived on Earth or will be living in the future.

Leonardo Da Vinci, Wolfgang Amadeus Mozart, Alexander Pushkin, Johann Sebastian Bach, Tchaikovsky, Lev Tolstoy, *Michelangelo, Rembrandt van Rijn,* George Friedrich Händel, Alfons Ven, "Abba", Elvis Presley, Rimsky Korsakov, *Albert Einstein,* "Enigma", *Galileo Galilee, Nicolaus Copernicus,* Nostradamus, Tesla, Mendeleyev, Marie Curie, Louis Pasteur, Stephen Hawking, *Jan Van Hyusum, Jan Davidsz de Heem, Edward Grieg,* Peter Breughel, Pierre-Auguste Renoir, Frans Snyders, William Shakespeare, conductor Igor Golovchin, actor Jack Nicholson, opera singer Vecheclav Osipov, father of wave genetic P. Gariaev, child prodigy Akiane Kramarik, Connie Talbot ... *you can add any creative person you know...*

3

Table of Contents

List of dreams:

1. VIA GOS CAME INSPIRATION, April 25, 1998
2. BIG CREATURE OF A HOLY RELIGION, October 31, 1993
3. BUSINESS IN THE CENTER OF THE GALAXY, July 16, 1991
4. THE GUIDE OF MY LIFE, February 22, 1996
5. THE BELT BUCKLE. THE LAW OF TIME, March 16, 1992
6. THE EARTH CURLED UP, February 12, 1992
7. A WARNING FROM THREE ASTRONAUTS, March 22, 1992
8. THE DRILLING FROM BELGIUM BOTHERS ME, October 16, 1992
9. YOUR COSMIC SISTER, March 20, 1992,
10. A MAN OF THE FOREST – HIS NAME, December 13, 1991
11. THE VIOLET FIELD OR THE STALKER, May 8, 1998
12. HIEROGLYPHS ON THE PALM, SEPTEMBER 12, 1992
13. THE UPPER KINGDOM, October 24, 1993
14. I WAS VERY THIN AND EXTREMELY TALL, February 11, 1997
15. ATHARVAN, October 13, 1989
16. ZARATUSTRA IN WATER, September 6, 1993
17. HUGE WOMAN ON A CUPOLA-SPHERE, January 31, 2005
18. A MESSAGE FROM THE MAGNIFICENT MAYA PEOPLE, June 24, 2008
19. LUMINOUS BODIES OF PLANTS, January 8, 1992
20. RUBY EMERALD, February 11, 1988
21. KUKULCAN (HUMAN-LIZARD), September 19, 1991
22. STARSHIP WITH FISH SCALES, October 21, 1991

Kukulcan

Chapter 1

Parallel World

There are many unexplained events that official science does not accept. Even when facts are telling the opposite and support what happened. What to do for the ordinary person? Believe it, or not?

How about if we pose the question: whether such phenomenon is *normal, natural* to our world?

According to the philosophy, the Law of unity and conflict of opposites, our world contains many pair of contradictions.

This is life and death, day and night, black and white, good and bad, normal and abnormal.

Let's check one of these opposites: OUR world and the parallel world.

The world in which we live also can't exist without his opposite – the invisible parallel world.

The scientist Ziolkovsky wrote: *"Material did not appear at the beginning as dense as it is now. There were stages of more rarefied material, when beings (entities) were created, which, for us are unreachable and sometimes invisible. However, they can be near us. If this is true, it means that thin rare-field material, much older than denser, younger material, then, of course, can be ahead of us in their development."*

Scientific proof of this statement exists: if we take together all physical objects on Earth, their weight does not equal the weight of the fixed mass, which it should be, according to the simplest of calculations. Therefore, it follows that this extra, lost Earth mass belongs to the invisible World.

Many do not believe in this invisible world. But radio waves are invisible, right? And we know that they exist and even go easily through the walls of our homes and carry particular information.

The ultra thin parallel world by its very nature is another non-material form of existence, the lives of intelligent beings. And their abilities are much more extensive than those of human beings. One of the characteristics of these living forms, in this invisible world, is that they show themselves sometimes on camera films, which can fix the radiations invisible to the human eye.

Here is just one case: A photographer from a local newspaper, in Ogden city, USA, Andre Rittenhaim, took a photo of an accident when a Cadillac ran into the car of the 32-year-old, Wilma Kenner, at high speed. What he said about this tragedy was this, "I took a few photos and ran to the laboratory to prepare them for the newspaper evening edition... When I looked at the still wet photos, in all five of them I saw a four-meter-high figure with hands like wings, between the flames and the black smoke!" He was shocked and couldn't believe his own eyes! Independent researchers have verified that these photos were real. (V. Lotohin, Secret Doctrine, # 16, 2008)

In order to study this parallel world and its characteristics, the Italian scientist, Lucian Bokkone, built a laboratory on a hill – it was an abnormal electromagnetic zone. He took photos of the empty corners, of the internal space. He built a special mechanism monitoring this space so that nothing could interrupt the process. This way it was absolutely impossible for anyone or anything from our world to intrude in this place. He obtained thousands of photos where there were images of strange geometrical figures, some entities, which do not exist on Earth – ghosts' contours and so on, and so on. Such materials made by many independent people exist throughout the world in huge amounts. Therefore, during its long history, humanity has lived near a parallel world. Sometimes the borders between the two worlds can open and visitors come into our world.

A friend of mine had his photo taken at the wedding of his son. The profile of his late wife is visible in the left hand corner – in the rainbow. It is the same woman which is on the photo on his lapel.

Kukulcan

*(You can see it better in COLOR at
http://www.ameliareborn.com/Photo Gallery -> book # 3)*

In this amazing case, the deceased mother had enough energy to attend the wedding of her beloved son as a Spirit.

It is important to know that the level of energy people have, and collect through their lives is one of the reasons they were born here, and they need this energy in order to survive and continue developing in the Spirit world.

So try to collect energy, don't spend it or waste it in ordinary stressful situations – fighting with your better-half, for example, because you both will end up crossing the veil one day. Enjoy life instead, and experience pleasure from spreading happiness, making people around you smile. Try to be creative with anything you do, in any kind of jobs you have.

What is the nature of YOUR Soul or Spirit? What happens to YOUR SOUL after death? When this life is finished, will it be the end of everything? Or is it only one little step among many that a person has taken already – walking through the chain of lives, still having many to walk in the future?

The devil, Lucifer, the prince of destruction, of darkness and ugliness is not the one who created people. God created people to be *Creative*, pure of heart and thoughts and to try to do the best they can to make this world happier, brighter, cleaner and more beautiful by their mere presence (EXISTENCE).

There will be a time when each and every one of us will die and will go to the Spirit world and reap the "harvest" of this life which has just passed. What did he gain?

Maybe lots of new knowledge, new abilities, skills, appreciation from the people around him for the gift of love and happiness he imparted to them? It will be an astonishingly sad moment for someone who will deeply regret that he did something wrong during his life: for his family and the people around him. Or maybe with his power and intellect, he initiated the huge destruction of a society, country, or nature on the planet!

Maybe someone tried to make money and acquired fame and fortune – an "image" – during his life, while destroying forests or oceans, or a whole country, and killing many people. However, then, he will be sitting in line waiting for his judgment with empty hands, because he just couldn't bring with him money or anything from his life to that place. Perhaps he will feel that he was sadly misinformed! The devil simply tricked him, attracted him to money and material possessions which became a "big thing" during his life. He spent all of his energy working on it very hard, but the real "gold" is now in someone else's hands – in the hands of those who were creative and improved their positive quality... how unfair, he will say!

"What goes round comes round..."

After reading my book, "The Priest", dreams, it will sound and feel as if you won't be losing so much after death. You will only shed one of the shells and it will be easy to find another one and to be reborn again, right? YES, people have many lives.

In one of my dreams, my late grandfather told me: in common life a person tries to succeed in something, to reach some level. But this is not important on the Other Side! The spiritual part which people collect here is almost not valued on Earth but very valuable out there.

Kukulcan

As I understand it now, Spirits and Souls coming to Earth are born again here to experience more, to receive a special kind of knowledge, which they can receive only here on Earth, for their development, ultimately moving to the next higher level in the Universe. One of the happiest days in this evolution is the completion of this cycle of reincarnation, birth, death, rebirth, forever stopping. Spirits are then elevated to the top of this perfection stage, as in the case of the 33 Spirits, who worked with the Brazilian healer João Teixeira da Faria.

João Teixeira da Faria is a medium of extraordinary capabilities.
His mediumship enables him to take on, or incorporate, thirty-three entities, all of whom were remarkable people during their own physical lives. The entities are spirits of deceased doctors, surgeons, healers, psychologists and theologians who are of such high soul elevation they need no longer reincarnate to our physical plane. They do, however, continue to elevate in the spirit plane by the extent of their benevolence and charitable works.
João's behaviour. (The Miracle Man: The Life Story of João de Deus, by Robert Pellegrino-Ostrich. Extracted from his book Published in 1997, ©1997/1998 All Rights Reserved).

In some instances, I feel a serious responsibility towards giving you this knowledge and prepare you a little for what you can expect after your own death. People are born alone and die alone. This responsibility and obligation, which resides in me, maybe, comes from the Ancient Maya Priest who comes to you now through thousands of years, to assist you in your plans.

It was his and my daily job to take care of people, their spirit's well-being during their lives, and to help them navigate their way when they cross the veil to the after-life.

I saw some dreams and I have a feeling that there is a time for enormous changes coming to the Earth; no one knows right now, what will be the outcome of these changes in the end.

In my dreams the Earth's aura is deformed and stretched to one side. Many people have the same; their aura is stretched to one side.[1]

When the Earth will begin its repositioning, it will bring death to people who have this kind of deformed auras – no matter how much they have tried to prepare themselves in this physical world. The good news is that there is still time to try to fix your *soul*. I believe Akaija can help in some special, unique way to do this adjustment, (http://www.akaija.com) and so can the body-soul healer, Alfons VEN (http://www.alfonsven.org/)

According to the Mayas, 2012 will be the end of life on Earth. I don't think it will be a total end. It will be the start of a new chapter of life on Earth.

---

[1] A little-known rotational force called the "biofield" has been detected around living organisms and has a strength that varies with changes in solar activity, lunar phase, planetary positions and the Earth's geomagnetic field. After several months of observations it was discovered that the amount of the initial rotational deflection of the Biofield meter varied in association with the geomagnetic field. The dashed line shows measurements made with the Biofield meter and the solid line shows data on the Earth's magnetic activity provided by the National Bureau of Standards in Boulder, Colorado. At times of higher geomagnetic activity, the biofield also showed higher activity. It seems that the geomagnetic activity is the largest component of the biofield activity. (Buryl Paine, Discovery of biofield)

Kukulcan

But I can guarantee you that the Maya people were smart. For example, no one knows why, but in their calculations they were using cycles of 63 million years! As if they were ready to live forever. And I am one of them, by the way.

I was a Maya Priest, and I am trying to help you now to be prepared as much as I can, with my own experience, to share with you the story of this amazing journey of my Spirit through lives and to tell you that their present life is not the last one.

It is much more comfortable to die in peace, calm and smiling, knowing that you will be reborn soon again. I am sure you agree with me.

So don't lose yourself at the last, most important moment of this lifetime, before you die. You will live as a Spirit for sometime in Spirit world between previous life and new one which you don't start yet. How this Spirit world looks like?

In a wise, ancient Buddhist book, "The Book of Death", you can find details of the day-to-day navigation after death – what to do, where to go. When I read it, even though it is written in some very special Buddhist terminology, I understood and recognized everything described in it. It supports what I experienced in the Spirit world. It felt as if I were taking this information on an energy level, not in words and sentences. But I think for most people this book would be a deep mystery.
I instead invite you to similar places, which look like those places where Alice in Wonderland had her adventures.

This is another world where there are more than three dimensions. It is very difficult to describe, simply because nothing exists there that could compare to our world and our life! Also these dreams were translated.

I still hope that even through these obstacles, my readers can smell, feel and experience – "What it is all about."

Since I saw these kinds of dreams from an early age, I am used to them. My parents didn't have any idea where I was traveling in my dreams.

Okay, let's go now through the door, to the room where my dreams are waiting for you: In these dreams the Spirit travels to another multidimensional world. Spirit also contacted and met other spirits from our galaxy and other parts of the universe. My body looks and feels different in this other world. Instead of a body it was sometimes just one solid point or maybe like a pulsation of energy, with sparks of quantum particles.

Honestly, I just don't have the words and I don't know how to describe it. The Spirit world is full of amazing colors, lights, dynamics, and speed, which does not exist in our world. It is full of magic things, pleasure and joy and multidimensional occurrences, BUT it could also be very dangerous sometimes.

The Spirits lives on the edge of this "world". It is on the edge between Spirit's life and death – not human life and death. In that situation, if the spirit reaches death, it will be not only a real human body death; it will be much serious on another level. It will be the complete death of the Spirit. There will be NO MORE rebirth or re-incarnations.

These kinds of dreams repeated themselves, continued and developed with the same subjects for many years, over and over again. They are very detailed dreams and they feel extremely real, each time I woke up from them.

Kukulcan

Best to name it as a separated reality, according to Carlos Castaneda.

It feels as if I traveled and lived during the night in some very real parallel world and visited the same places...
I recognized people, Spirits and Entities which I saw, visited there before. I noticed the changes which happened to them over time.

It is impossible to say if it is the Spirit's life from the past or from the future. Or maybe it is a dimension, where past and future exists in the same place? You can try to decide that for yourself.

Warning!
I don't want people to think that I am crazy, so I asked a doctor to write something for me. Here is a "note from the doctor":

> *Julia did not belong in any mental institution. She is mentally healthy. Her outline point of view may be the result of a much higher IQ than normal and as a result there is a possibility for her to see the world a little bit differently than most people do.*

So let's take the first ride.

I classified the dreams according to their different levels of energy. If you feel that you are totally lost and don't understand where you are, just skip that dream and go to the next one. Yet, it is best to still read it. Even if you don't understand it, on the spiritual level or on your chakra, aura levels you will understand, accept and absorb this information and you might adjust to it. Not to worry: Your Spirit will take care of it.

I purposely put here the plainest, basic dreams, which I saw more than 10 years ago or around that time. At this moment I see myself at a more "advanced level" of cognizance, and it is almost impossible to describe it. I guess no vocabulary exists for this yet.

(You can find many more dreams in the complete version of my book "The Re-birth of an Atlantean Queen." www.ameliareaborn.com. Here is just a short version of them. These books are about a Spirit Journey through a chain of many lives. It is like a gift of rare knowledge, experiences about the existence of a much BIGGER Eternal, Spirit LIFE outside of the present one, one that each of us is living right now).

Dream # 1
Via Gos Came Inspiration, April 25, 1998

Something was deep inside me; disturbing, kind of worrying me all day long. I felt as if I would have some special dream that night or something unusual would happen. After all, I didn't know and until now if I was sleeping, or if it was real. Throughout the dream, I was in control and didn't lose myself.

It started with a terrible crashing sound. It was a horrifying thunder, as if the sky broke apart. It did not last for long. The sound could not last too long. But it was so enormous, incredibly loud; it seemed that I had never heard anything so loud, that my consciousness divided this sound in several parts. And I thought that I knew how to divide it and to play it on an instrument. It was a boiling, roaring sound. In order to describe the thunder during the storm..., it begins, then increases and should stop abruptly. And there were about four of such sounds, one after another. They started approximately at the same time, the last one was the concluding one, the loudest, and then it would be just one thunder sound.

Kukulcan

It seems to me that I even sat in a bed. And then I saw myself, like it all happened on a computer screen. The dot is flying forward, as in a game, the airplane is flying, and there are contours of mountains, etc. I understood that I was that dot. On Earth we have gravity. But this was not a fall; it could be compared to a fall into a bottomless well. It seemed to me that I saw the contours of rocks around me, but I was still falling. Such a depth, such a long distance.... As soon as all this cracked, my consciousness rushed there, to the bottomless well, but I was not falling; it was not a downward movement.

I don't remember how this movement ended. But there was a qualitative change. During all of my dreams there was only my mind – no body, no arms, nothing. There was nothing from reality, yet at the same time, everything was real, life-like. I said life-like, but actually it was on the edge of life and on the verge of death. After that night my self-perception changed dramatically. I lived at least two parallel lives. No questions. No doubts.[2]

I can only compare this with the army, when they have maneuvers, they shoot with blanks, but here it was real, not some maneuvers – huge dangers were lurking – you had to be on the alert all the time. It was like that. And yet there was nothing terrestrial – no fields, landscapes or rocks. The only thing I know about it – there were lumps of space, so to speak, they were different. It was

---

[2] Peter Gariaev's experiments show the DNA of each person makes a photo of their body, its surrounding situation, what this person sees and senses and is sending it to the universe every single second! It is some information exchange going on, some connection, adjustment with someone, who is also you, who lives there in that parallel world. Maybe each person on Earth has his twin there. As for me I can prove it with hundreds of dreams where I am always two in one.

happening in phases; each phase differed from the next by a time period of my staying there and by the tests that I had to pass.

I understood that I was not there for the first time, but many, many times already. It is a tension on the edge of your capacities, on the limit of limits. Once I heard a voice – it was not a human voice, but a female kind. Like a fairy. It was a round sound. I remember it, this voice. I remember her. She was a kind of owner of this space-lump. I got there and she said, "You forgot, you were here already." She guided me and I remembered how I should operate in this space; I remembered how to avoid these few dangerous traps.

At one moment, I jumped into something like... you see your chair, imagine that it is circular and there is a wall a half-meter high alongside the circle. So I sat there – although I did not have a body. There were several of us there. Someone, a male beside me said, although without words, but I understood, that it is necessary to compress quickly. There were such super-heavy elements around us; I had to twist somehow, to become a monolith. He said, "Now those crazies will come. They're like children, who will try to pull us apart...." Later, it started to shake, to pull us apart..., to try to rip us to pieces.
All this is hard to express. It was happening in fragments, space by space; each of them had its own pattern.

"Via Gos Came Inspiration." This sentence was pronounced loudly during the last stage; it was a lasting, loud sound. Like a crashing sound with which all this began. No idea what it means...

Dream # 2
Big Creature of a Holy Religion, October 31, 1993

Today I fell asleep. The dream in its reality was very close to what has happened in Caracol. Not life, but very real. Sometimes it seemed that this reality is stronger, than real life. Distant reality – it is right. I was different; there was a different sense of self. I was very concentrated, like one strong crystal, or a monolith, with one and only goal in life. There is nothing besides that, nothing at all.

I haven't seen such concentration in life. In real life a person needs to eat, to drink, to redo something, etc. One depends on the real world, depends on sustaining oneself. I would call it our "friction of life", inertia. It does not exist in space where there is no gravity. And I had only one desire – I was walking and I knew that I should fly now – very far away, very, very far. Unbelievable, but it was my goal, the essence of my life. I was living by it all the time. The place, where I should fly – maybe some galaxies... I know exactly the place and now I feel it. There was a very, extremely important thing to do. In my dream, I remembered, what it was. But even in a dream it was impossible to describe – everything was hanging on very delicate feelings. The dream was attuned to this harmony.... It would be like the astronauts walking to their spaceship, knowing that they will get in and will fly with enormous speed to unimaginable distances.

And my goal – even if to speak about saving the whole humanity – would not be enough. Something global and serious.... And I alone should do it. Just by myself without other people or assistants. Only I can perform this task. And this desire is concentrated in me and I am arriving to the moment when it will drag me there.

My goal was very distant – I was from there, from far away – as if I knew from where – I could get there easily, to that distant place. But my goal was from there, I came from there to perform my task.[3]

And, strangely – there was nothing in my dream that concerns our world, the Earth – no grass, no people, no buildings – only myself, my concentration and the path – like the white Milky way, I just see its direction, feel it.[4] I must enter it and to find myself there. And

---

[3] It looks like I used this Black Hole for the travels in Space, when I was a Mayan Priest.

"Mayan hieroglyphs describe it as a " Hole in the Sky", cosmic womb, or " black hole" through which there wizard-king entered other dimensions, accessed sacred knowledge, or toured across vast reaches of the cosmos. In September 2002 astronomers verified the existence of a massive black hole in the Center of the Milky Way, naming it "Sagittarius B." Jenkins writes about it: "If not a coincidence, the dark-rift itself might indeed be the surface signifier of deeper cosmic mysteries, ones that the Maya were well aware of." This black hole is "the cosmic womb from which new stars are born, and from which everything in our Galaxy, including human, came" (Daniel Pinchbeck, 2012 *The return of Quetzalcoatl*, 2006).

[4] The black hole found in the Milky Way, December 9, 2008. There is a giant black hole at the centre of our galaxy, a study has confirmed. German astronomers tracked the movement of 28 stars circling the centre of the Milky Way, using the European Southern Observatory in Chile. The black hole is four million times heavier than our Sun, according to the paper in The Astrophysical Journal. Black holes are objects whose gravity is so great that nothing - including light - can escape them. According to Dr Robert Massy, of the Royal Astronomical Society, the results suggest that galaxies form around giant black holes in the way that a pearl forms around grit. Dr Massy said: "Although we think of black holes as somehow threatening, in the sense that if you get too close to one you are in trouble, they may have had a role in helping galaxies to form – not just our own, but all galaxies. " The researchers from the Max-Planck Institute for Extraterrestrial Physics in Germany said the black hole was 27,000 light years, or 158 thousand million miles from the Earth. "The most spectacular aspect of our 16-year study, is that it has delivered what is now considered to be the best empirical

suddenly there is some creature in front of me – a human being, a Spirit. It had no face. I just can compare the importance and responsibility with my concentration and appropriateness – like Saturn, nothing unnecessary. He appeared in front of me – straight, clear look, strict lips, if for a moment only I could compare *it* with a human face.

I knew him; I knew him well. He said to me without words (telepathically) – as if asking, "Today you will not fly to that distant goal" (This injunction is not ruled by anything, it does not depend on anything; it is like, today it is raining and tomorrow it will snow.) He said that today I should participate in SOMETHING ELSE. It is like in a Milky Way there is a side branch which has a real ending and I need to help someone there. He expressed it as a request. It is a short and direct injunction. My main goal, the task of my life – *will not disappear, it will stay forever.* He had shown me this other aim for me to participate and to help.

I turned up in a place with some other people; we were like astronauts in the second film of "Aliens" where they all lie down into some cells to fly this unbelievable distance. It was like an airplane turbine, white, frayed sides, the hole, the entrance. We entered into something white, shiny, huge, with soft edges. We entered and then it felt odd. As if my body came out of me – the body, the heaviness, everything that has inertia, the weight was lifted – released. Only finest thin spacesuits, one over another remained – of incredible lightness. Perhaps only the soul stayed. Very, very light emptiness. They were transparent membranes, like Medusa's; I don't remember how many – 5, 7, 10. I

evidence that super massive black holes do exist." Professor Reinhard Genzel
http://news.bbc.co.uk/2/hi/science/nature/7774287.stm

started to look at it – at what I was wearing. It was like a spaceship, the whitest, transparent; it could be compared with a fluorescent lamp but it should be the cleanest one. I thought *what a beautiful spacesuit I have! It shines like silver.* I knew one thing clearly – these few others and me – few human creatures (I can't say "people") selected among all people, as many as those who lived on the earth. They are a unity, a whole, sublime, light, holy..., not exactly a creature – one holy business, one religion, super-religion, superior. These few people... you know, the superior beings have something that unites them – some beings superior and sacred. The same was true in this instance. As if there was one superior creature, maybe a principal that had chosen us. And the selected ones – us – decided the future of the people in general. They are above people, as if an extraction of all people was performed, like something single and big over the earth, something great that unites all of the people. They guide it, they know what to do with it, and have a sublime sacred goal. I don't know what to compare it with. And today I could not do what I wanted. He said that today was a special day that we should come together for some session. I felt that these few people were in the same situation as I was – they were wearing hoods. We all got into such a dream, but I was not sleeping and I had control over my thoughts; I can't understand it, they weren't sleeping either. We were in a kind of antibiosis with one thought or direction for the work we were to perform very clear in our "minds". There was a feeling that this living religion became one creature, acquired qualities from most of the living creatures. It was thinking and acting independently.

In different occasions I was dreaming in colors, in *living* colors every time – once in a few months, or years. It was an event, and I remembered it – the whole period of life – green-poisonous-emerald, rich blue, orange-peach, pink, bright raspberry, white and light-blurred blue. But it is improper to list them; they are beautiful and LIVING colors. And today – a great revelation – it was a living energetic creature. Her energy was spliced of fine rays of every creature, infinitely clear and sublime. It is made of all these colors. There was a feeling that there were no people below us – just a single cloud of all the people. They govern it; they want to affect it with this religion. And today we had to fly away from the Earth. This big capsule started to twist like a swirl, the tunnel appeared, we were flying through it, and there was a sensation of permanent twisting. We had to fly to such a place. They were doing something with us there.

I also remember that I was tall, high, maybe three meters, or more. I was wearing only white. We arrived to such a place, a very distant one, although while we were flying very far in this capsule, it seemed like a moment. But when we arrived and stopped, nobody was coming out, we were hanging – and the most important thing was happening there, something very global, crucial – and it took a long time. Something was happening to our spacesuits, or raincoats. As if I shed them off and became very light. And self-perception also changed; when I woke up later it was still going on. They were doing something to us; the sensation of lightness increased, the crystal – it was me. The longer it was going on, the stronger the feeling of lightness became.

These dreams that you already read and this next one, belong to the same Spirit, which was in Amelia's body before – during my past life. Amelia Earhart acquired this strength, concentration, and this enormous focused goal to fly all over the world from the deep roots and the experience, which her Spirit accumulated during previous lives as a Mayan Priest, an Atlantean Queen and others.

Dream # 3
Business in the Center of the Galaxy, July 16, 1991

I had something to do in the center of the Milky Way Galaxy – just don't laugh. I recalled being there. Our Earth is very far on the side. I understood that I go there quite often for business. You know, my body is very different – it is not soft, a tender-skin body like here on Earth. In fact, it is like a lightning. I am on Earth for some very pressing, but very short business. From there our Earth appears like a "rational" slime. Before, at university, when I was studying squirrels, I thought that they have a very complex system, an almost human body, but, in fact, this is all terribly primitive.... And now, I understand that you absolutely do not need to develop your physical body, you should only maintain it. And it is not frightening – to die – it is just to leave the Earth. They don't have senses there – it is a rudiment. They come to Earth to study, experience it.[5]

---

[5] Yes, an astrologer told me that this is possible, because my ASC in my astrology chart is connected with the Centre of the Galaxy! WOW! So, I am flying there for some important reason, not just to have some fun...

Today is November 22, 2008, five months later, and I decided to write something here, because I just woke up, again, from an enormously powerful dream. I was flying with astonishing concentration and at an incredibly high speed to the same point in the Universe. The little doughnut-guide was near me again, talking very fast, as usual, in his metallic, computer-robot voice. Information, words were dropping one by one like a million of little beads out of *him*. I tried to write this down. At the end he told me, "You are the real 5th element to humans and this is an important point for the Earth's history. Get rid of all frictions, which take away your attention, for the next few years, from one goal: to make *"the way through smoother"*." Anyone has any idea what it means maybe? I feel very strong tension, almost

Dream # 4
The Guide of My Life, February 22, 1996

(This is a short version, the full version of the dream can be found in the book, The Re-birth of an Atlantean Queen.)

In a dream there was my guide. I asked him, "Why don't I want to receive information from the surrounding world, about progress, science etc. anymore?"

He told me, "You should not worry about it – if all the rest does not disturb you, then this also does not. It is at a level of gods and their representatives on Earth. You know everything and more than necessary already."

As if I was living in the 21st century, but I am from the 25th century. This is not new, but old for me. And I remember that I had such sensation in my childhood –

---

pain in my "time-travel-belt" point right now. I am sure the Conclusion at the end of the book will help you dramatically. I recalled that in my dreams I visited some top nuclear physicists regarding the study of the smallest known particle, it is so small – it always exists in a non-exist form – that it is simply impossible to record its presence. I have an amazing idea how to use this quality and with the help of my company, SSF technology, using Tesla methods, I propose to devise a way to "smother" our planet during 2011-12. In my dream I asked these scientists the key word to find them. As soon as I woke up I dial in Google and ... found real people! I called them instantly. The last team I called was from the Institute of Physics and Technology of the Russian Academy of Sciences – Physics and Astronomy.

PS: "size" doesn't really exist in the way we think of it on a quantum level. There is "no" experimentally verified radius for the electron or any of the quarks. As best we can tell, they are point particles, occupying no physical space. Neutrons and protons have "size", i.e. seem to occupy physical space, because they are quarks held together by the strong force, and so their "size" is simply the range at which the strong force interactions between the quarks dominate. So, the smallest subatomic particle doesn't exist, as subatomic particles don't really have a size.

of insufficiency and emptiness, of sadness – insufficiency of the world around me, of nature, of people, of society – everything was primitive.

****

Attention please!

People who can not understand my dreams and still don't believe that life exists after death will be very surprised, instantly after they die, they will still be "alive", but in a different way. And now in Spirit world..., what's next? What to do? Where to go?

Just go directly toward the white, brightest glowing light where there is an open door leading into the beautiful heaven. Where I went in my past life.

(You can read about it in the complete version of my book, "The Re-birth of an Atlantean Queen".)

A cardiologist from Holland, Dr. Pim van Lommel, proved that the Soul lives forever and consciousness does not depend on the brain!

He checked 344 patients after they came out of their coma. Consciousness continued to function after the heart and brain activity stopped.

In one case, when a patient, whose heart had already stopped, when the ECG showed no brain activity, and before artificial ventilation of the lungs was applied, the nurse took out his dental prosthesis and put it in a box on the desk nearby. When the patient returned to life, he waited until that very same nurse came into his room to remind her that she took his prosthesis and placed it on the desk – she had forgotten about it. He said that he saw everything that happened, who said what and who did what in that room from the instant he *lost consciousness.* He said he was watching everything from above – on the ceiling. The same doctor also proved that it is not an oxygen deficit, which creates the pictures of the tunnel in the mind. Because from 344 patients, only 18% saw the tunnel – if the lack of oxygen was the reason, all 344 people would have seen it. He thinks that the rest of the people probably needed more time for their Spirit to come out and start traveling towards Heaven.

Dream # 5
The Belt Buckle. The Law of Time, March 16, 1992

I woke up three times; the dream was going on. I was feeling this belt on me. The buckle was like a case of an audio-cassette. The belt was thinner, narrower. The color was beige, like my skin (it was as if soldered into my skin). The buckle was made of white plastic. When I woke up for the third time, through my sleep, I had a feeling that thousands of eyes were watching my body and their "sight" was directed to the belt as if it were golden threads. From every little eye, there is always a flow, always a sensation from all the spots on my body.

On the belt buckle there was a round button, closer to the left side. On the buckle, there was also a vertical crack. Something had to be inserted into this crack and something protruded out of the belt in order to insert the thing into it. The crack opened and closed.

After the third awakening, I remembered only one thing – I understood time. *Time does not exist without space. Objects are defined in space. The presence of material object creates time.* The fact of the existence of material objects in space creates time. All three of them assume that this object should change (develop, evolve or devolve). As soon as a material object disappears, the un-evolution (or devolution) ends.

Where there are no material objects, there is Eternity. I understood it very clearly. I tried to change time – forward or backwards. If I pulled time in front of me, I stood in place, but moved time as if on a slide-rule. I don't remember the process. It was always connected with the belt – I was doing something with it. At different times, I unbuckled it, buckled it, and pressed the button. The buckle was like white fog, like my smoky stone. I don't remember the belt clearly. If there is such a belt, then there should be a buckle. One, which is also me, my second self, had shown me such things, explained to me and taught me, and I knew that it was I. She was speaking with a resounding voice into my ear. The lower part of my body is a "galactic disk" – a very thick, humming disk, but it is a thousand times denser, concentrated energy than what I described in previous dreams, and it can rotate like a weight at the gym. The upper part of my body – on the contrary – was extremely light and almost weightless. This part can rotate relative to the upper one. The second part – the upper one – is a transparent, radiating light; nothing specific can be seen – everything is "blinking".

***

In 1899, in Arizona, workers digging the ground for the construction of a future hotel found an ancient burial made from rose-marble blocks which connected to each other so precisely that it looked like one solid piece. Inside this "mausoleum", there was an Egyptian-type of sarcophagus made of a strange blue colored substance in the shape of a human figure. The painting on top of the sarcophagus was that of a giant man which was lying down. He was absolutely naked and wore only a big, wide belt. He had sandals on his feet and a crown in the form of an Egyptian miter. Inside the sarcophagus there were only ashes. All the items found and the ashes proved the ancient source of this, because over time the skull is the last to be destroyed. Well, maybe he had a belt to travel through the Universe during his life? The same as I used in my dreams.

It is interesting that the famous physics scientist and mathematician, Nadgip Valitov, who conducted several studies on the non-equilibrium structures, concluded that, in the future, there would be a possibility for conversation through time and for the resurrection of dead people! His work received international appreciation from scientists and even from high religious quarters, but he himself is a traditional scientist with down-to-earth materialistic views.

A group of scientists in Russia can send people back in time for a short moment. They are able to send people back 5 or 17 years in the past and even 6 years before their birth! There was a public demonstration of their assertion in September 2008. They invited five volunteers through the newspapers – you could apply directly until August 15 to participate in the demonstration. They wanted people from the public to be independent and to prove that it was possible. They guaranteed a safe return. Wow! It sounded unreal.... Well, I sent them a letter, but I was late to send in my application when I saw their ad in the newspaper. I still have this Science News newspaper with their ad! They sent me an automatic response that "this e-mail is no longer in operation"....

Nevertheless, I wish I could meet them and check how exactly they're doing it. I'd like to ask them to try to send me back 17 years in the past to see my mother again!

It would be a very exciting teleportation experience into the future or to another planet, on the condition of safe-return, of course. I feel, I know for sure, no doubt for me whatsoever, that this is possible with people and things, because in my dreams, I often see all things around me (trees, rocks, buildings) as a set of dynamic frequency vibrations or pulsations. I can "press" this frequency and "transform" it into a solid object or to do the opposite. For example, I can go through the walls easily, because I see them as a plasma or colloid with a special frequency. I know how to see, to make myself, my body as a frequency. I think it helps me travel very fast through the Universe – faster than light or sound. This is how I can send my body and frequency far away into Space to some exact place of which the frequency is familiar to me already. For example, I can go to those galactic huge bee houses where my "space home" is located. I guess this is how I travel in time. Because information is also moving at a particular speed in time, as soon as you break the barrier you move at a faster speed and you find yourself in the future or in the past.

About TIME

Let me say it again, *I see it like a spooled thread, rolling one over the other and the other, and each of them is a span of time PAST, PRESENT, FUTURE. If something happens in space, such as an earthquake, for example, or another problem occurs, and as a result a wormhole is created amid the threads of this bobbin, it can be easily understood how people, ships, trains or animals disappear in one place, only to re-appear in a different place at a different time – traveling from one time to another.*

I know that the human creation of long railroads with trains and tunnels forming giant fish nets of steel structures, hundreds of thousands of kilometers long, interrupt space and as a result time on the planet. This is the main reason for the formation of wormholes and an explanation why trains disappear and re-appear years later in many different locations all over the world. The famous case of the small tourist train from Italy which left Rome in 1911 and went into the longest tunnel in the mountains of Lombardi and never came out of that tunnel, is a perfect example of this! Since then, the train was seen in Mexico City, and afterwards in many countries during our century, and finally even in the new tunnel under La Manche! Well, imagine how people in that train felt – frozen in time for almost 100 years! I hope they were all happy not knowing that they were stuck in time and would be living forever aboard that train!

According to the scientist, Pazei I.P., railroads are also powerful energy information channels. Any algorithmic movement creates an information flow. For example, a few years before this train disappeared in Italy, there was an earthquake near Massena. This event could have created not only cracks in the land but also it could have created a wormhole in space which was moving around the tunnel. Since the movement of the train was connected with the railroad, the lost train could have appeared in any place conditional upon the fact that there would be a railroad on site at that time or one would be built there in the future.

The "ghost trains" hit and killed many people on railroads every year in very strange and unusual circumstances. Witnesses tell that people were killed near or on the railroad when no train was around. Or the "ghost train" suddenly appears out of nowhere and creates accidents.

Last year, on September 15, 2007, a man was killed, smashed into little pieces on a small, country railroad. When the police found him, there was no explanation how this could possibly have happened. Obviously, he was killed by a train, but that railroad had not been in operation for the last 20 years! No train could travel over that railroad because it was broken in many places and rusty! (A. Vasiliev, "Miracles and adventures")

Another mystery: two years ago now, two bodies – a man and a woman – were found on the railroad near the city of Novgorod. The woman's body had been cut in half by some old train which was going at slow speed. Trains like these just do not exist there. All trains in that place are traveling at speeds of 90 kilometers an hour and in case any of these trains would run over a person, only little pieces would be left in its wake.

On June 14, 2001, the minister for railroads transport of Turkmenia, Hamyrat Berdiev died on the railroad! According to the witnesses, he was standing near the railroad when he was suddenly pushed onto the rails by some strong power and killed seconds before the train arrived and stopped close to him. It is interesting that there was no blood, no parts of his suit had been disarranged, and there was no sign at all of any contact between the train and his body. So please remember that rail roads are very dangerous places and be careful. There is always the possibility of being killed by the "ghost train" or disappearing in a time hole.

I travel in my dreams, through time, to the future and I made lots of predictions along the way, which have come true.

Here are just a few examples of the technological developments, which I saw in my dreams since a young age and later became a reality.

In 1980, I dreamed that I was in an airport. I went to the TV screen on the wall, touched it and entered the data from my diary, which I had left home in another city. I did some writing, closed the screen and went to the gate to board my plane. In 1980, personal computers did not exist yet, and they were certainly not available or accessible to the public. As for the internet or transferring one's diary from one terminal to another, was beyond anyone's imagination. However, now, 28 years later, you could go to any airport, use your laptop, your phone, access the internet at any "internet café" and access your diary wherever you are in the world.

In another dream I am in some field far away from town – it is some kind of sandy desert. I have a phone in my hand, I start dialing and called a girl, who suddenly appears in front of me in three-dimension – a hologram – and who starts talking to me with a clear voice. It was absolutely real, except that I put my hand *through* her and could not *feel* her – the space she seemingly occupied was empty. I decided to check the date at which it occurred – because I remember the exact year, how old I was at that time – the dream was on the night before my birthday! It was thirty years ago. Cell phones did not exist at that time and I did not see "Star Trek" until I moved to Canada in 1990.

Last year my business partner, Anthony, who is a very smart and open-minded entrepreneur, introduced me to a very interesting researcher in the Department of Surgery, at the University of British Columbia. It was an unforgettable day, meeting the Professor of Surgery, Dr. Karim Qayumi, Director of the Centre of Excellence for Surgical Education & Innovation (CESEI).

He started his research with a study of the memory and later found that medical students remember only 10% of what they studied during the lecture after they finished medical school. Students remember a little bit more when they also read the material and much more when they practice what they have been taught.

Memory depends on one important factor: how many areas of the brain are activated – sound, vision, movements of the hands, problem solving participation and so on. He found that the best results were obtained when the students participated fully in all of the activated memory areas. Dr. Qayumi created an interactive computer-assisted instructions program that looked like a video game in which students visit their patients, define the symptoms, diagnose the problem and perform real surgery.

During our visit I had the opportunity of performing a surgery through this computer-assisted program – right there on that day. Imagine this – I had no idea what to use to make the first cut. There were many instruments in front of me! The computer navigated me through the process and instructed me as to what to do. Brilliant! The students are usually performing three surgeries a day. Even grade 12 students study on this program, very successfully.

Doctor Qayumi is an amazing and very talented man. He even created robots for the students to practice their surgical skills. This robot lies down on the operating table, in the operating theatre – he looked like a real person to me. I felt his pulse and observed his breathing. After giving the patient an adrenalin injection, I observed that his pulse started racing at an incredible rate!

I had mixed feelings at that moment. I didn't know who would run first – me from the room, because my patient seemed to be very agitated, or him by jumping off the table and running down the hallway. I asked, "Will he stand up and run out now?"

"No," the professor replied, "but if we give him a bigger dose he will die, his heart will stop!" Well, what could I say?

At that moment, when I was near the robot, I remembered a dream I had many years ago, and related this dream to Anthony.
In that dream, I arrived at a company to receive what I ordered from them.

My order was a boy. There was a couple – two old people who ran the company. They came out with him and started showing me his abilities. We went through the whole list of them which I ordered from the beginning. He was excellent, he looked perfect, and he smiled. I made a note that he also had very positive emotions. I was happy with the order and paid them extra.

This boy was a robot boy. I ordered him to do the work at home: cooking, cleaning, teaching my child and entertain, give medical diagnoses in case a member of my family was sick and prepare custom-made food for each of us, with minerals, vitamins, and apply creams, give a bath, a massage to the ones who needed it, and so on. He was to be that special someone in the family, who cared for everyone – someone which we no longer employ these days. He also had some secretarial responsibility.

In the house, there was some special sound healing room with specific vibration...

I remember, on the way to the car, I stopped and looked at the peacock walking around in the garden. He looked so beautiful that I tried to decide if I should order one like this as well. The bird was also a robot, you understand.

When I returned home, I found that this dream occurred 24 years ago!

Well, I expected that all of this would come true during this present life. I have a reason for this. My friend, a genetic scientist, opened the code of longevity and proved scientifically that people could live up to 800 to 1000 years now. He started his research many years ago and observed that some people even started "a rejuvenating process". In one case, a 76-year-old grew five brand new teeth! I saw the X-rays of her mouth myself. Amazing!

Once, a professional astronomer asked me about the location of the planets, and of the stars and I described everything in infinite details – not only the location, but also the nature of these objects, their atmosphere and so on. It was a surprise to me that everything he told me – what I had said – was absolutely correct. On top of it, I even added more details that, at this moment, are still unknown! This little episode should demonstrate to you that humans have unfathomable abilities. Our spiritual body, as some people call it, this astral body, can travel during our dreams far, far away ... and collect information.

****

Once, when I was in South Korea, I visited a place, outside Seoul, named the Cultural village. While I was there, the locals performed a special Korean traditional dance. When I watched it, I just could not believe my own eyes! These men had a long white rope on their hats and the entire dance was dedicated to that rope.
I am sure most of you know that we all have an invisible, thinnest thread, which connects our spiritual body from the top of our head to our astral body during sleep. No matter how far we travel through the universe

Kukulcan

in our dreams this thread still continues to connect our astral body with our real body, which we leave sleeping in bed. The entire population of South Korea is Buddhist. So it looks like this knowledge about the thread is basic there, and that they even have traditional dances dedicated to this silver thread which shows the kinds of qualities it has! Amazing!

Korean traditional dance

Dream # 6
The Earth curled up, February 12, 1992

I saw the Earth, large, huge. I felt its enormity; it was occupying all of my scope of vision as if from the cosmos. The Earth started to curl up inside itself. It was happening very quickly. It is hard to describe with words, but it was easy to watch. Initially, there was a cutting in the Earth in one place and the peel started to roll inside, like two rolls of paper, rolling in opposite direction from each other. It rolled in and disappeared. I did not see it anymore. The line of the cutting was drawn across the Atlantic Ocean, between Europe and America, diagonally. Before rolling up, the Earth turned into a blue colloid sphere, as thick as condensed air, and when the sides were rolling inside it, you could see one layer through the other one. When the Earth was rolling inside itself, it looked like a bright-red, burning ball.

I saw a few dreams like this regarding the Earth. Another dream was on February 5, 1988. According to that dream, the Earth will be "broken". It will have cracked at first, after which it will be wiped out. It will be year 1695.

As you can see in my dreams, I know the time when events will happen and the exact year when they will occur. But these dates are given according to some other calendar system than the one we use right now. Maybe someone knows and will tell me? It could give me a clue as to which civilization I once belonged and from what kind of culture this calendar is. Most importantly, it would give me an indication as to when this will happen to our Earth.

Kukulcan

For example, according to the Zoroastrian (Fasli) calendar, we currently live in year 1369. So we have about 326 years here on Earth to prepare to move to some new home on another planet. It is possible that this calendar is the ancient Zoroastrian, because I see the Persian Goddess very often in these dreams.

By the way, I feel really uneasy. It is weird to calculate such a global thing as when our mother Earth will be wiped out... 1695 – 1369 = 326 years from now. It is a very, very sad, enormously heavy feeling.

****

Today, three weeks after I wrote this, my friend gave me a magazine and there I saw a short article: "Hawking says we must go into space." So I decided to add it right now, before my book went to the publisher, to calm my readers down.

I will type only a short part of it:

"...Stephen Hawking says we must go into space....We are not likely to be able to stay on Earth much longer. The possibility that our planet will be wiped out, Hawking believe is quite significant. The good news is, if we can avoid killing ourselves for another century we should have the necessary space settlements in place to launch our descendants into the universe" (reference: Atlantis Rising, magazine, number 59, page 13; "Hawking says we must go to space").

He continues:
In 20 years he thinks we can have a base on Moon and within another 20 years a settlement on Mars. To find any place else "as nice as Earth"; we will have to go to another star system.

Sadly, I think this is the best option, because in previous dreams, I also saw a problem coming with the sun....

Sixteen years after I had this dream, Mr. S. Hawking supports what I saw. It is nice to know that we have some extra time and that my channels are open to receive information so clearly.

But I wish it will never, ever happen to our beautiful, amazing planet Earth and it would have been just one of my weird dreams.

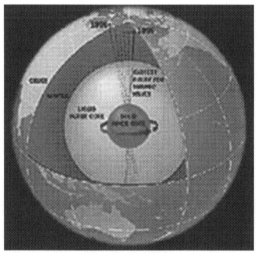

Earth inside

PS:
Predictions about our future can move forward and happen earlier than we expected, because of the disasters and the time experiments on the planet and because the creation of time wormholes continues. At first, *The Philadelphia Experiment,* then *The Montauk Project,* and now this *super-collider* under Switzerland which can create a black hole ... and swallow our Earth, the way I saw it happened in that dream.

Kukulcan

Today, a few days later, I found something else to add here!

M. Nostradamus and Ranio Nero both independent from each other, of course, predicted that humans will move to space, because it will be impossible to continue living on Earth in future. People will build cities, which are similar to a chain of huge balls, beads – it looks like a jewelry necklace. *It will happen in year 2200.* Wow! I am close with my prediction. If what I predict, that Earth will be wiped out in 326 years, we had better move out ahead of time. It is best not to wait another century as *Stephen Hawking* advises us.[6]

I saw our planet, Earth, in my dreams sometimes in different dimensions. I saw one more continent. It was long, like North and South America together, all in one piece, not divided in the middle. It was not as wide, half or a third narrower. I guess it was located in the same area where the Earth started cutting and after the peel started to roll inward, in the *Dream # 6, The Earth curled up, February 12, 1992.* The line of the cutting was drawn across the Atlantic Ocean, between Europe and the whole North and South America, diagonally. It's like a spine of the Earth with the row of mountains there, on the underwater, long, slim continent.

I remember visiting this place from time to time, walking there. I liked a few places to the North, it will be Portugal and part of the African level, but I avoided the places located further south, close to an equator or below. I tried not to go down there for some unexplained reason. I felt danger looming in that area. It is a kind of

---

[6] In order to reassure my readers, I wish to tell you that Nostradamus' prediction about Earth continues after year 2300. His last one concerns people coming from rainbow clouds and belonging to year 3797. Next he wrote: It is not given to me to see beyond the year 3797.

space filled with wormholes which could swallow you like quick sand, absorb you forever. If this is what Atlantis looks like, this place is located on the same level as the Bermuda Triangle area and down, where airplanes and ships disappear. At the same time, if in my dreams I was walking on the continent where Atlantis is now located, under water, it would explain why it is grey and foggy down there.... Sometimes it felt as if you were visiting someone's country and you would have to be on your guard at all times, hiding, on the alert.

I visited one pyramid there; this is my favorite. It is glowing with a blue light, very deep in the ocean; it is black and dark around it and I just don't know the source of this light. What worries me is that possibly, in this part, which was left after Atlantis disappeared, there is still an active process going on, something like a radioactive reactor, some kind of Atlantis broken power plant which might create a huge wormhole that could be the reason why Earth would curl up in this area and be wiped out. Yes, I wish to resolve the mystery and I wish that scientists would ask me, under hypnosis, what happened with Atlantis and about this underwater pyramid!

In my dreams, I saw how this giant mountain chain, this spine lifted, raised out of the water and splashed enormous waves onto Europe and America. It was a huge disaster.

On the other side of the map of Atlantis, which I saw during a hypnosis session, it looked like the shape of Antarctica, but smaller. I saw a capital city on the northwest side. Maybe there were big climate problems around 10,500 years ago on Earth. As a result of the pole shift this island, which was part of Atlantis, moved south and is now Antarctica. There is an interesting connection between Antarctica (possibly Atlantis) and Turkey (mother land of Sumerians). The Turkish admiral Piri Reis drew maps of Antarctica without ice in 1531! It was 300 years before it was opened. His sources were ancient maps and plenty of information which he found in Turkey! Well, it looks like the Sumerians from Turkey and the Atlanteans had a connection and were some kind of "business partners".

Dream # 7
A Warning from Three Astronauts, March 22, 1992

I was in a big hall and someone was telling me (there were no people around) that three astronauts from the other planet arrived on Earth. They wanted to warn us, or to say that our sun got into a period when it began to fade, and later on it would shine like the white nights in St. Petersburg or on the North Pole, but with much less intensity.[7] It would not glare and there would not be any shadows. I saw the Earth immediately – how it would look – the animals, the trees – in a different light.... This phenomenon concerned something serious, something global for the Earth. The astronauts got interested in one thing which was hanging over the Earth – the shape of a three-leaf clover (three-hexagon). This one thing consisted of three separate parts (elongated in form). They were like gusseted rocks that you find on the beach.[8] The "message" was important,

---

[7] Changes in the Sun's Surface to Bring Next Climate Change – spaceandscience.net, Jan 13, 2008. Today, the Space and Science Research Center, (SSRC) in Orlando, Florida announces that it has confirmed the recent web announcement of NASA solar physicists that there are substantial changes occurring in the sun's surface. The SSRC has further researched these changes and has concluded they will bring about the next climate change to one of a long lasting cold era.

[8] This summer my friend gave me a book. It is the story of an amazing boy, Slava Krashenikov, who was canonized by

unusually important. The form or quality of these planes was of a great interest to them. When they approached (maybe in order to investigate them), they died. I saw them when they turned up near the "thing". I saw three planes, three astronauts. It meant some kind of law; I knew it in my dream. The "thing" was of sand-gray color or yellow clay. When I woke up, I knew for certain that some astronauts perished on that day. It was deeply sad. And the day before, a word came to me – "Triangle".

Later, in my dream, I saw a huge asteroid coming to the Earth....

Maybe we should pay attention to the messages we are given. It cost these astronauts their lives...very sad.

Russian Orthodox Church as a Holy Man. He died around 10 years ago at the age of 11. During his life he had the miraculous ability to heal people and he made thousands of predictions that later came true.

While I was reading this book, I suddenly found his prediction about the same triangle shape object in space near the Earth! Here is how he explained it: When space rockets return to Earth they bring with them some special, almost invisible light-grey, yellowish crystals from space. It was "built" like a bee hive, like a gusseted rock in one of our atmosphere layers. This crystal grew fast by itself and it represented a great danger for the people on the planet. Due to some conditions, which will be created by people, it will fall down and destroy everything on which it lands. The crystal will look like an icecap that will not melt. The good news is that the "crystal" in question will fall down over Siberia where isn't much population to speak of. From the time this crystal attains an enormous size; it will fall down and will grow the shape of a two-leaf clover put together – six-hexagon. Well, I saw it, the last time, 16 years ago; I don't know what kind of shape it has now...

The problem with most people is that they are afraid of what they don't know or can't understand and they start creating some "funny" theories. It is just their way of trying to save people from what does not even exist. I wish to elucidate, to put this mystery box on the table and open it. I wish to let those hidden "secrets" jump out and show themselves to people, because in reality nothing can actually hide – there is nothing on Earth that should provoke such unhealthy reaction or attract such a distorted attention to the facts.

Dream # 8
The Drilling From Belgium Bothers Me, October 16, 1992

I was talking about myself. Here I am, and there is the other one, who is talking about this one: I have a clear channel of communication. But clear is an inappropriate word. Clear means that when it was un-clear, they washed it and it became clear. Here it is not so. There should be no dirt at all. It is crystal clear. As when you say, "I have it crystal clear," but something is interfering with your hearing. This drilling, this interference, in my dreams comes from Belgium, from Europe. In a sense, it is not a war, but they are trying to interfere with my dreams. And about me, she started her talk with the words, "She is eternal."

****

Nostradamus, in his prediction "Centurii", he tells that he sees, in Belgium, some centre of ancient magic... Well, it looks like this centre still exists or, when I am in my dreams; I am crossing the same path with them.

46

Dream # 9
Your Cosmic Sister, March 20, 1992.

In the first part of the dream, we were tracking down these creatures. We were in a Cosmos, in a capsule; we were floating. There was a Guide, but he did not participate. We were communicating, but not with words. I did not see you and the Guide, too, did not see your bodies. I knew that you are near me and talked to you. Not with words. I was teaching you. I brought you up to my usual walk, like a *stalker*. Every time everything is new. Everything is focused, I am like a warrior. All my attention was concentrated on tracking down these creatures. Besides which, part of my attention was directed to you, teaching you. You do not see it and I feel with all my cells. I felt that they were approaching to us in spasmodic, dashing stages. We were there a long time. I told you, "I feel them..." We entered space; we felt each other mutually and were coming closer. I taught you how to feel. I myself was on the verge of feelings. I was telling you about all my sensations. Maybe they were already beyond many planets away from us – it is something different, they are the others (but we also were not humans from Earth, we were from some cosmic civilization). They were – from the other one.

At some moment it started with increasing force. We were rushing at enormous speed, but the distance was so huge, that it took a long time. At the beginning, I felt them just with a feeling, and then with another feeling, then a third – there are no such feelings on Earth. It was like stages. When the fourth stage came, I knew clearly who they were. That this was a highly organized civilization, that there were several of these creatures and they were trying to establish contact with us. I recognized her (maybe they also have females) and I said, "See! Here comes your cosmic sister!"

Kukulcan

At the last second, when they were in front of us, I recognized her; she was very close already. In a few seconds, there was a whirlwind before us. When I understood that she was *your cosmic sister* – it was like a forgotten past or like a silent knowledge. Maybe I knew her as far as billions of years ago and maybe I never knew her. I said, "Be prepared! Look!"

It seemed that we were decelerating and we managed to see each other. I noticed you were on the right of me; the Guide was behind – like a triangle. Like children's inflated swimming pool – the shape of our positions. She seemed to have two representations – like a knight in armor – she had a narrow cap, helmet as if made of small plates.[9] I had a vision that we were passing some mansion with a path; I saw and felt it. Suddenly something like a flame – like a dog, or a red fox, like a splash – like a comet with a tail – flew out on this path. I knew that it was her. She flew to meet us and grabbed my hand with all her force. The left hand. It was a strong and unexpected *physical* sensation!

---

[9] When I see the symbol of the FireFox program on the internet with a fireball and fox with a burning, orange tail, I always remember this dream and the chain of them I had. Everywhere this orange fireball fox repeated itself – always touching me, mostly catching my hand.
I just received letter from a Belgian woman: *I dreamed about you last night and the overall theme was: connected by the light and flying through space... it made me very happy, I have had many past lives, also in Atlantis, Egypt, etc., so no doubt we know each other. Marianne Notschaele-den Boer*
http://www.vorigelevens.nl/
When I clicked to this website, I saw a photo of the "cosmic sister", my cosmic twin! My body was shaking and covered with goose bumps, we reunited in real life16 years after I met her in my dream traveling in space for ages!

I woke up immediately. Because of this sudden awakening, a strong wave hit me in my chest, like an explosion. I even had a rush of fever. I should not have been awakened. When I regained consciousness I had the feeling that she was still holding my hand, that they were there, waiting for me to fall asleep again. This sensation moved towards my elbow – seven or eight centimeters before the joint. Later on, I could not fall asleep because of this sensation in my arm. And now I understand that in order to bear such moments and not to wake up it is necessary:

1. To have a lot of energy;
2. To saturate your life with unusual eccentric sensations, in order to satiate your body, so that your body will not be surprised.

Dream # 10
A Man of the Forest – His Name, December 13, 1991

I could not fall asleep. I was looking at my watch as if I had an appointment. The previous time the watch showed 12:30. The nap lasted only one hour – when I opened my eyes, it was 1:30 (13!) – one hour or 58 minutes.

When I woke up, I understood that my dream had been repeated twice. A half hour each or it was a recording in my mind and it played twice. Everything that was happening and was there, despite the fact that I dreamed it twice, was like a fog slipping out of your hands. It is really hard to translate it into words.

I was on the Earth; maybe I was in a parallel life, in the world which is very close, but not the Earth – best to name it a separated reality. I was in some space (we say apartment, but it is a rough definition). There was a Guide, who spoke; his voice resounded during my entire dream. And also there was my great-grandmother whom

I never saw before – nice, small and incredibly wise. It is like that on Earth – people live, each one in his own way, and then they come together, something unites them, this convention. If I flew there, then it would have been "because it is not from our life," said the magicians. But in this life I don't do it like that. I do something and also I live somewhere. It looked like a seminar - there were separate essences; it was like a report about how to live and what you do. I was saying this and made a conclusion, the others did it, too – although it was just my report, perhaps.

Those (the others) were several; I don't know how many. What was happening with them, I cannot describe and even understand. These creatures differed enormously. There was one – I think she was female – the Ying Chinese symbol. To be near her you should have been careful – I don't know how the others protected themselves. She aroused interest, but at the same time she was deadly dangerous. I was like seaweed in water, but like a chameleon changing my qualities, but faster than it – or appeared and disappeared, or produced rays – it was a kind of pulsation; I don't know what kind. It was dangerous for everybody. Everyone was also pulsating, but it was of another, different nature. People have a body, face, breast, back. And there was a creature which was at my back – something behind my back, light, fibers, energy – had to be situated perpendicularly to the other dangerous creature. Something was behind my back, if it stood straight – it should be hanging over it. Something of mine was being placed over him. But maybe it is necessary for him to understand my words – and I have an object from my body which I can hang over his head. It is hard to explain . . . I am just trying.

At the beginning, it seemed that there was an attuning to each other going on..., and something else which I

50

don't remember. Maybe there was the third one, everyone was telling something. And afterwards there was the fourth one. When I was talking, maybe I delivered information without words. When I finished, I heard the voice of my grandmother (I just heard her, but did not see her). She knew that it was valuable for them, but I did not understand – she told them this and that. But it was not from our life. This reminds me of something like *Jabberwocky* in Lewis Carroll. I understood, they understood. But here I cannot understand at all. In *Jabberwocky* there is a substantive and adjective. But here there were neither of them. It was an event from my other life. The others were listening and were correcting at the same time. While I was telling my story, they were absorbing it. One perceived it as green, the other like an action, the third one flicked out something, and after that they started to exchange; each one perceived the fine facet that only he could understand. And after that they produced a synthesis. All this was in the other sphere of life – not life itself. Later another fragment arrived, when the human conversation started (before it was soundless, the humming Guide was translating) and I transcended to human rank. It was as if I consisted of many stairs. I reached them on the top stair, the same as theirs. On the first one I was attuned, and then a stair below, when we were doing something together. Later, one step below, again – when I was telling my story. It can be said that stairs are material. When I was telling a story, it was almost human; there was an action, energy, matter. On the last step, there was a human being. I disintegrated into several creatures, and later – into myself-human. And on the last step, the voice of the interpreter appeared; it was a translation into human language. I even thought that this Spirit dictated to my friend's psyche – he fitted by rank, position – he understood me.

Kukulcan

I remember what they said in the end – they said it two times and when the dream repeated – again two times. Four times altogether. They pronounced with a loud voice (the interpreter said it, because they could not speak) for me to remember, "THE MAN OF THE FOREST ... HIS NAME..." – with a thunderous voice, loud, fearful, the loudest in the world as if a mountain began to speak. It was said loudly, solidly, strongly, like an elephant's walk. I don't remember what it was for. I cannot know in my human condition what we were talking about and I don't know, what is happening with this "Man of the Forest". I already opened my eyes when it was pronounced for the last time. They woke me up in order for me to remember for sure. When I opened my eyes it was: 1:30, December 13. 13 and 13.[10]

****

The dream described below is the longest dream I have had thus far. I named it the "Violet field" or "Stalker". This dream is for someone who has the patience to read it – it is pretty long. You can easily skip some parts of it and still be safe, avoiding the dangerous trip to the violet field, which is full of temptations... "It was on the edge of something larger than death."

I am visiting that place from time to time. I don't know my goal for doing this, but I guess I am looking, hunting for the real deal: "Deep Quality Danger Spots" on our planet and in space in order to exercise and continue to develop my Spirit.

---

[10] 13, interesting! It is an important number for the Priest and a lucky one for me in this life. It showed once 3 times on the license plates of the 3 cars arriving one by one, when I tell my friend, Istvan, that is an important number for me.

Dream # 11
The Violet Field or the Stalker, May 8, 1998

Today, it was real, palpable, on the brink of every imaginable danger. I do not remember all of the details and oddities now.

I woke up at 3:00 a.m. Weird dreams always happened at three o'clock – I would wake up at 3:00. For me, it is usually time to enter the other reality. An extraordinary state would engulf me, worry me at 3:00 a.m., when I was in my cozy home in Gorki-10. Nobody disturbed me there. I could control my sensations.

There is an odd Zone. It can be compared, in modern language, to virtual reality, an unusual one. Nobody would put on special glasses to visit it, though. I simply step out – and I am at the beginning of the road, and I start walking. I know this road, I am aware that there are three levels of complexity on this path.

The first one is the Fore-Zone, and then there is the Zone itself. Inside this Zone there is a remote site representing the purpose and the meaning of the whole Zone. In my mind, the name of this site sounded like the "Violet Field". It was a sensation of incredible danger, of distant definite end, of unbelievable difficulty of reaching this end, and, at the same time, there was a sense of attraction to the Zone. For instance, a person lives this present life and then transcends not into a different person, but into the same being at a different level. It's impossible even to compare this to a caterpillar's transformation into a butterfly. It is entirely different – a mutation, a transfiguration, a sensation of violets growing very dense, extremely dangerous, blossoming on the edge between life and death.

Kukulcan

However, since there was no life in this dream, it was on the edge of something larger than death.

People were flowing in this direction, constantly – one by one, two by two, and groups of them. I saw them walking the first stretch – only the first. Nobody returned from there. It's rare when somebody comes back. They lose their minds there, they lose their self, and they lose their identity. They dissolve into nothingness. The Thing devours them. I can tell from experience – I have never seen anybody coming back. I have seen only those coming towards me – nobody returning. I know that they stay there, dissolve, the Thing annihilates or destroys them. It would be ridiculous to say that the Thing "eats" them; the Thing is too grand for this, too ingenious, beautiful, and people are only tiny insects compared to its "magnificence".

I felt that this was real, that it existed on our planet. Perhaps it is our astral world, where individuals with extraordinary psychic abilities could enter. This reality sucks them in; it is made for this purpose. They enter it in their meditations perhaps.... Afterwards, they cannot live in our reality as people, as persons. One should have a very strong core, stronger than all of these enticements. A certain entity – intelligent, energetic, of divine power – has created the Thing. There are lures and temptations everywhere. They hold a person there. Everything is based on unusual matters that can entice a person away, so they would forget their essence, forget that they are human beings, and forget their structure. Everything is arranged to infatuate a person, to make them lose themselves, then the Thing swallows them up. For example they say – "he's going mad." He doesn't remember himself, as if his mind or brain has been pulled out.

This road looks like a forest road – it's smooth, trees on one side, sunshine seeping through. Cars never drive along this road. There are two footpaths: one is ascending, the other descending. One should climb up and up, all the time; walk with effort on these paths. It is smooth, but one has to make an effort to travel these paths. The central, even road, perhaps, just divides ascending and descending footpaths. This is the first section of the road.

During a conference this summer, an incident that occurred then comes to mind, which relates to this dream. I was sitting at a round table when suddenly; I passed out and found myself in quite a different place. I recalled this very place today – the smooth road, the sunshine seeping through the foliage. I cannot remember now what happened next, I was totally out of it. The women next to me hadn't noticed, for some time, that I was unconscious. I hadn't been sleeping. Everything disappeared immediately for they shook me back into consciousness and asked, "What's wrong with you? What is it?" Today I recalled that it was the same place with the same rays of sunshine, the same weird atmosphere, oppressive air, special energy.

When you approach the Zone's entrance, there are guards standing in a row stretching to the horizon. These men in uniform look like military-men, they all look alike. They are dressed in something austere, black perhaps. They make up a fence preventing people from wandering outside the paths. I have approached them many times; three times I have entered and walked out. When I saw ascending people, I snickered to myself, "They will notice the guards now and will think that it's real." I knew for sure, that all this was unreal – this being created everything. People are trapped from the very beginning. Those guards are a border between states.

Kukulcan

I have no idea why nobody else knows this fact. The Thing created everything in the Zone – all these oddities and extravagances within it. In fact, it doesn't exist. That is, it does exist, but the Thing controls and constantly changes it. It is evolving and moving. I have an approximate map of its location, in my mind; I know how to reach the *Violet Field*. It is a large stretch of land with a piece of seashore inhabited by weird creatures. But the sea is without depth and continuum. I remember all of the details and nuances of this Thing in the morning and during the night – when I have the dream.

After that – the Bald Hill. You could meet lots of people there. They attained an incongruous size somehow. I knew one creature (it can be called a woman, I think), maybe I have met "her" briefly once. I know that I have entered the Zone many times and have addressed her, but this woman wouldn't hear me, wouldn't recognize me; I hadn't had any opportunity to help her. This time I saw her again for a fleeting moment. Now and then I could see something in her eyes, as if she had recognized me, but she was not sure from where. All her memory – of her previous life, of me, of herself – had disappeared; she didn't remember that we are all human beings. This time, when I was passing by these weird creatures from the sea, I spotted this woman on the Bald Hill. It is always windy on the Hill; a whirlwind is always swooping over the top of it. The Hill is not very high, just trampled down into a balding shape; those creatures are constantly rushing about up there. They are not beings, not human beings. There is not much space there, but protuberances sprout out and turbulences are speeding about all the time, thus all the people there are moving oddly fast, whirling about, like constantly moving, flying objects, at great speed within this restricted space, non-stop. Each of the creatures has something like a shoot or wing – a triangle, similar to a sail, larger than they are – a precise triangle that looks like a boomerang, or a moon crescent on its back. I hadn't got such a thing for I was not a lost soul. The rest of them had dissolved already, but these were still rushing about between heaven and hell. I was aware that their conscience was full of those ethereal creatures around them.

I realized with astonishment (I was awake) that within an hour I visited the place, let's say, three times. When I was there for the first time, I had seen this woman but done nothing. The next time I saw her, her glance reminded me of something. Once I arrived to a small town (it was two weeks before my departure to Canada) and met a girl, who greeted me, mumbling something without changing her facial expression; she didn't recognize me, couldn't grasp my existence, her glance was wandering vaguely. Probably people on drugs look like this. Now this woman's stare reminded me of this girl's expression. I've made an enormous effort to help her out, beyond the guards' line. In fact, I rescued her. Let's assume that four years of my life in Canada have passed between my second and third visit to the Zone, but my dream lasted only an hour!

She wouldn't recognize me, wouldn't grasp my presence. Her glance was wandering helplessly, unfocused, noticing only those chimerical creatures around her. I could see her consciousness in the shape of a medusa, which doesn't have anything solid in it, everything had been dissolved. I started throwing sand into this consciousness; to help these dispersed molecules regain a reverse memory and to restore, to rebuild its lost, inner fragile structure into something remotely resembling the previous one – to shape it into a tree with branches, to create the inner star which unites the jellyfish-like brain's outgrowths, to create a skeleton from it.

When all this was organized, then she started to see and perceive me. She had such a perception of me – it happens with religious fanatics – she did not respect me. They respect and worship only this essence that created this wonderland. She was still fanatically faithful to it. But at this moment she could feel herself as a separate being, like a grain. The separation had happened already, although minimal, from this terrible creature. I pulled her out in such a condition, with great difficulty, and left her alone.

Somehow, the ones who lost their minds were very heavy. It felt as I was pulling a long train, a machine weighing tons. While they are in the Zone, they become laden with an indescribable burden. It is not clear how these heavy creatures could swirl on such a small piece of land. They fly up and down with their wing. They do not slide on the ground; therefore, they have more space, in all directions. They are moving in the streams. It is strange, and hard to watch. This Thing is pulling them around; they do not belong to themselves.

I had my own goal. My goal always is to get through all the unusual and strange things that come across my path and not to lose my way, to feel intuitively this *Violet Field*, to come to it. It is a very complicated, very difficult task. I'll explain why. The qualities of Virgo are very important things in life. I looked at their plan from above. I was smiling to myself – I knew all the tricks of this "madam", this very cunning creature. I knew that she was doing it for the benefit of better prepared persons like me. She changes all the time the inner disposition. She does not change everything, though; otherwise a person would begin to feel lurking danger and concentrate. She does it cleverly. I needed to go through long *Furrowed Fields*. A person is walking, taking the usual route. He has been here many times. He does not notice the matters beside him, although they would attract anyone's attention, indeed. He knows that beyond the *Furrowed Fields,* there is a glass – the White Palace, which I called, for all intents and purposes, the 'Laboratory'. At the entrance, there is always a woman dressed in white. What is behind the laboratory? There are different things; white stairs, the woods..., thousands of different things. He keeps this in mind, the plan, and everything in its place, just slightly changed. Yet his plan becomes worthless already; he goes by the wayside....

The laboratory is made of light glass, as a glass palace, as the cosmic UFOs, as described by witnesses. At the laboratory's entrance the woman, in white clothes, waits for you and then guides you inside. You should pass through a lot of labyrinths inside. There is a room of rooms, room of rooms, in which there are various and frightening creatures – frightening by their unusual appearance, variety, attractiveness, fearful incomprehensibility. You don't know what they are, it is impossible to understand it with your mind. They are frightful because they always stop you. They always attract attention. I always stop in front of each of them, and this contact between us is like a struggle between them and me to overcome them or at least to stay equal. To bear their influence, it takes three to five minutes – to pass this test. You cannot circumvent this building, and you cannot avoid these creatures.

Two of them caught hold of me strongly and *absorbed* my condition. They brought an indescribable horror into my soul. I knew, that I was dreaming, that it was a created reality, so I decided to imagine this road full of these soldiers, to stop my journey, and not to allow myself to wake up right away. First, I had simply to come out, and wake up after that. It was important. I don't remember how many times it happened prior to this one particular episode. Yet, I remember how many times I reached this clearing, perhaps I never came near it. I made a decision, that now I should get out of here immediately.

At that moment, this line of soldiers and this road appeared clearly, in my mind's eye – before my eyes. Maybe, I don't know, maybe I had not come to it, maybe time after time I went farther and farther inward, getting used to these substances, trying to get through them farther and farther – it seems like it. Since I passed the Bald Hill easily, the sea, the fields with blueberries, I knew their dangers, specificities, what exactly is dangerous about them. For the first time there were these two essences; I had a really good look at them and I survived their contact.

They were in one room, on the right and on the left of me. I was allowed to enter the laboratory and this woman brought me in (usually she was only at the entrance, and I thought, *this is something new*). Maybe there are a few of them, they all look alike and not one of them is authentic. How talented, a genius, is the one who invented them! It is beyond any rational thinking. You can't absorb it with your mind, with your senses, with your intuition ....

They looked alike as if from one family. They did not have anything, which could be referred to as fear on Earth. Usually you can recognize your enemy by its features – when it is a vampire, or predator, they have fangs, tentacles, poisonous saliva – everything that attacks you and ruins your body. They had nothing that ruins your physical body. I don't remember my body, by the way. You could accept with your mind that they were in two *aquariums*. They certainly were in a watery substance. Let's assume that these aquariums were suspended in the air – as large as a room – such an aquarium, and every one in it was filling it almost to the rim. They were about three meters high, but their power, strength seemed not to match; they were even stronger, more powerful.

Then there was a form of salutation, when golden rays – millions of golden rays – came out of a spherical point. There were a million rays; it looked like a jelly-fish. But if the salute was golden when it shot above water, it dissolved into a fog of stripes, as black smoke going through water, as streams of ink from a squid, but they did not disappear, they remained in suspension in the water. But up there, on top, the spherical point had merged into a myriad of these stripes – unmovable billions of stripes. There were not any movement there; no sound, no color practically, no sense of physical density – was it hard or soft – no parameters by which to describe it. Between them there was a difference in colors, the other one was darker and denser. I was horrified by the second one.

There was a difference in what they were sending to me – what defines the meaning of their existence. It was like a struggle, torture at the verge of my … strength, I cannot say nerves, since nerves exist only in real life. I stood in front of one of them at first, then in front of the other. I approached her, to face her, very closely. There was no other way. It was a conscious move, she felt me very strongly, everything I represent. That is why her knowledge about me makes her stronger and gives her an opportunity to affect me selectively – in those areas, where I feel her. She affected me even more – she concentrated and put pressure on me.

There was a constant flow, which comes from her to me. It comes but does not approach, because it came in pulsation. And here – it is like a field, constant field, it pulls you. I was not frightened of the fact that it pulls me, like the others; I entered and approached to a certain distance from which she could affect me, but to be in her field was a hard test. There was no fear – they all are unknown, incomprehensible, so to speak – it is the first stage, where the water is....

There are just strange forms and it attracts people. Here the forms are unimportant, and they capture you deeper; they penetrate, test you, and evaluate your human structure. Maybe something which is beyond intuition? I don't know what this feeling is, what kind of sensation a human can experience. But to be in this field felt like unconscious fear, horror. You are in this condition and do not know what it may bring you. This condition is unbearable; it is on the verge of ... of all capacities. The only sensation I remember of me was that my solar plexus was attacked; there was pain, severe pain. There was a very strong physical tension after strengthening my loins and shielding my being. I felt as if I had used all of my energy – I was spent – and decided to return. But later – it was so strange – I came to another room and went to sleep again.

There were two of them – the initiators that led me there, they knew – and a third one who just tagged along. I looked carefully at this small person (people appear pathetic there, insignificant – not because of their size, but because of their inability to cope) and it seemed that it was a girl I know ... I remember ... I evaluated them – that they are unable to get anywhere, that they would not come back. But this one I knew and she seemed to recognize me. And what did I do? I returned. I entered into that Zone with them, walked them to the edge, showed them a little, and took them back. I had shown them – only from the side – what is there and how it is, and I marked on somewhat of a plan that there, on the right of me, diagonally, straight from my shoulder was the *Violet Field*. Perhaps when I entered, I always looked from above. Immediately, I thought, "Oh my God, I was here just now, but everything had changed already. The Furrowed fields, the Sea, the Bald Hill, the Cranberry Plantation (like in English parks – they cut labyrinths), the Laboratory, and there is a mass, a million of different things." I just realized that these initial things, which existed from the beginning, had changed already. There are no fields anymore, or they are moved aside, and in their place, there is something inserted – the *clearing of solar prominences* (fiery gasses which interact with each other). It is like a mosaic, but there is, say, a hundred colors and variations, and here they are endless. You should always remember what was there before, what has changed, where it was before, to evaluate yourself, if something new appears, to evaluate this new thing and yourself, your capacities. You should do it, in order to define if you've passed three new zones, but ten of them you may be incapable to pass. The plan, like a map, is retraced with everything in repeated renewal.

When I was coming back with that non-authentic girl, I saw from the corner of my eye, that those who had followed us did not come back. And I was holding her all the time. I photographed the first third of the route in my mind (I could not capture it as a whole) – and it had changed – very cunningly changed. So to pass through it all, you need to remember your goal, to have a sense of the *Violet Field* and walk through it with your eyes closed. And once you got used to it, and you recognize something, everything is familiar. You walk and walk, and then suddenly, you will stray off course.

It always feels as if an undefined anxiety envelops you while you are in the Zone. Time changes all the time there – with the changes of mosaics it twists, it screws and with it the fields drop out, then they appear again. The principle of appearance and disappearance – they do it by changing time. Space and time is one substance, you cannot separate them. You are once in the past, then in the present, then in the future. You get from one thing to another with temporal changes. There is no future or past – it is just different times. It is not linear, as on Earth; it is unintelligible to me and it is frightening, inexplicable. There are some lapses constantly – you walk straight, and then suddenly fall into another pit.

The sea is conditional. It is not something going far into infinity. It began conditionally and finished right away after coming to depth – instantly. There was a million of different things, creatures, expressions, movements. I can say only one thing – all this was soundless, and colorless. Maybe everything there was gray-white-black. There were not any shades of color. Some kind of an astral world where there are no colors. The only things that had color were the violets. They were of a deep violet color. I remember it with my eyes. Then again, I don't think that there were any flowers there. Perhaps it was some surface, substance into which you enter, up to your ankles, and in which you stay, some energy-like thing ... but it is, I know for sure, situated on a flat surface. You should enter it as you would a field. Maybe it radiates energy upwards and you stay in it like in the *aquarium*....

There were elements – like water, like wind, hurricane, and fire. There were time lapses. Everything was happening in some space, where some flows, unintelligible to your mind were not linear, not in three-dimensional space, but more-dimensional. For instance, those lost souls on the Bald Hill, you could see by their movements, what sort of field was there, what kind of streams. Everybody was walking there – they were attracted to it, like someone is attracted to greed, greed to possess a treasure; they either knew or felt it, they were drawn to it. When at the beginning they walked this thorny path, they walked in all consciousness; something interested them, maybe they had a presentiment of the *Violet Field*, but they did not anticipate the hardships that were awaiting them. They were drawn as if by a magnet, like flies to honey.... They wanted it very much. They all walked, driven by an impulse. They had only enough energy to come to the soldiers, but not enough for more.

My strength was in knowing, in feeling, that those ones were not soldiers, and the water was not water – that all of this was not real, not genuine, that it does not exist. The danger resides in something else.

***

The question is HOW it is possible to remember such a long dream?

I also had another dream about it and I decided put it here, in case if someone did not read my book "The Priest".

Dream # 12
Hieroglyphs on the palm, September 12, 1992

I was sitting on the hill, the hill of yellow clay, leaning my back against the hill. There were similar hillocks around, the size of about two meters, not more. Some oval form. I realized that I looked at my palm, the left one. There was a drawing on the palm – a sign almost as big as the palm. As if it was stamped by a stamp of a very good quality. There were no chiromancy lines on the palm. There was a white rim, like a closed circle. And some colors. Such colors are painted on cakes –

65

meringue – rosy, protuberant and dried on. And it was like that; each line very clear and they stuck out over the skin.[11] Apart from white, there also was red, and, maybe also brown-beige and black. It was a three-dimensional, complicated figure. The lines did not merge, as if they were drawn under a microscope. It looked very much like a hieroglyph, but a hieroglyph is always based on a square frame – this one was rounded. At least one side was curved.

I was looking for a long time, and then I saw two women approach me, they looked like they were from India, wearing clothes of a fabric with streaming, iridescent pattern. I recognized them. I said, "Oh, I haven't seen you for a long time." I said, "Look, I have a sign," and stretched out my hand to them. They started looking. (I remembered all this with difficulty, as if through thick honey, or layers of water; every word was hard to utter.) They also said about me: "You are a Goddess, and there is also one more person."

I asked them, "Where are you, where are you coming from, what is your life like?"

They said, "We can show you," and laughed with a rustling sound. "You probably should know yourself."

They said, "Because you have capabilities, energy," (specific energy in dreams).

I know I am used to make a plan, and remember everything in my dreams. I break everything in my dreams into parts, fragments. And I have a capacity of automatically storing in my memory major moments,

---

[11] The Maya word Tlappalan means land of red and black. Black, red, brown-beige are the colors the Maya usually used for their tattoos. All tattoos on the face are flat drawing, but they are as if embossed over the skin surface.

coordinates. However, since I was 16 then, I always threw out of my memory all the unnecessary information and I controlled my thoughts. They knew this. And they told me, that if I wanted to, I could keep all of my dreams in my memory. And I could wake up, coming back to them years and years later.

They said, "You will see and remember all of the details, every hour." (And this will enable me to change the past and the future – if I would go to them often then I would see and remember the future more clearly.)

They also said that people cannot remember this even if they get there. And this would make no sense to them, and they would not get their experience there. From that comment, I thought that maybe people do not have enough energy. If I knew which step brought me to what, then it would become possible for me to plan my own life and change my life.

****

Now, here is a very interesting and perhaps the most important dream in this book.

Dream # 13
The Upper Kingdom, October 24, 1993

Part 1 – the clash

It was some terrible, black, big and hairy creature. I was feeling it. It was approaching, coming closer to me in order to kill me and some of my cute creatures, who were standing behind me, behind my back. I realized with my mind, that the beast was approaching but it was still far away. I went with my creatures to the woods, through strange brushwood, they were not woods, or bushes – they were just branches growing right out of the soil, interwoven, like barberry.... and white sand; they were growing on white sand. I brought my creatures to this THING. Then something crawled out to meet me. It had green spots all over his white body. The wise one. It appeared, suspended in front of me. It was speaking with a soft voice, like Kaa (the huge snake in the cartoon about the Indian boy, Maugli). It said to me, "I will save yours, the little ones." And it began to unwind, unroll, as if it was crawling out of an invisible crack in the wall. There was an opening and it crawled out – I didn't see the inside of the place. It was growing in size – expanding, and became as big as a Hercules plane. From the tail, a huge crack opened across its body leading my creatures inside it. Its head was flat, like a leaf. The crack was in the lower side – and my creatures started walking inside IT. And here I saw them with my eyes, I knew beforehand that I had them; that they followed me, and the snake spoke about them, but now I saw them, finally. I was very much surprised.

There were less then ten of them, maybe seven or eight. They were little animals, different from each other, sweet, nice. Spirits or Creatures... I cannot describe them. I can not even name them. Once in my dream, I went with Kaliostro – there was such a tiny elephant, and a semi-plant – None of them walked, but floated over the ground ... the spirits. They were like spirits and similar to the creatures from another dream, which looked like that little magic hen, like those two birds, which are not really birds that were coming to me, such as that shaggy-haired one that lived in my castle – that's what they looked like. Very strange, no legs, no arms, just their individual essence – very nice, very cute. Then they started walking in a line, like children in kindergarten. They did not mix up. When they were all inside it, the snake closed up, curled inside itself, slithered behind the invisible wall and disappeared.

Then suddenly this horrible beast came upon me – to kill me and my spirit-like creatures. The beast had something very sharp – something between a scythe and a sickle in its hand. Besides that, he held two more sharp things – one like the sharpest arrowhead or spearhead, a lance maybe. The second weapon was a semi-round object, similar to a fishhook, which had been inserted into a wooden stick. Once inserted into the stick, you could not pull it out. It was easier to leave it there. But it was protruding from the stick slightly. I had a feeling that it was not supposed to be put on the stick *(or it was perhaps "retractable")*, because, when you inserted the hook in it – just *a print* in a shape of the letter   was visible – and no one could notice it. The other weapon had a heavy ball attached to it, similar to a spiked ball attached to the end of a chain. The sharpness combined with incredible heaviness made for a dangerous weapon. It was similar to a medieval flail – a spiked ball stuck to the stick by a chain.

Medieval Flail

His armor was round-shaped, curved. I was rather afraid of him. I would have rather run away from him. I cannot describe him – when someone comes to kill you, then you fix your attention on the thing that is supposed to kill you. He was like a blurred, dirty, heavy, wet woolen spot – a very hairy Siberian bear; big – about two to three meters high. But I knew that I should not run away, but defend my creatures, I had to fight. Then something surprising started to happen. I was looking at everything as if from some other, second sight. Suddenly there was two of me. Everything ended up very quickly – looking from the outside – incredibly simply and easily. The other me, who was fighting did this – she was standing away at about two to three meters and then the beast lunged in my direction – at that same moment, that same second, an air stream appeared in front of him, very thin, it captured him then lunged and turned in the right direction. In front of him, there was something invisible, similar to a veil with gold threads, fibers, but incredibly taut and strong, like laser rays, twisted. There was a breath inside the veil, or something like a stream of air, invisible. This was in the air in front of him right at the moment he lunged at me with his armor. He hit the veil around him. His body was pulled into the threads, bending around and twisting to escape. It turned up, he hit, cut himself. Meanwhile, I did nothing. I just stayed there and watched from the side. Yet I knew that I had created this air-wall with threads in front of him. And I noticed that the sickle, that had stricken him and was in his hands, looked actually like a laser disc, but larger, and incredibly thin and sharp.[12]

So, when this all happened – I was surprised, but the other me, who was doing all this, went and found it immediately. She knew where to look, where it was, I felt them – the other two weapons. They were at a distance, hidden in two different places. It is hard to

---

[12]   This is the kind of disks that Chak Mol had, (see the book, "Who is Chak Mol?" by Julia SvadiHatra).

explain; why they were there. I approached and found
the flail, without the wooden end, large – ten to fifteen
centimeters long. I went to the other place and – in a
strange small wooden construction, on the steps of a
small house – I found a wooden box that was not
touching the ground, floating in the air, just like the
first weapon. While they were in such a condition, they
were still dangerous – I knew this. I felt that I must level
them. They could be unloaded – and I did it.

Part 2, Palace, celebration

The dream went on. After I finished with the third weapon, I went to the palace, to check what was going on there. Everything that happened occurred just before the great, magic celebration. There was to be a feast of magical enchantment with the participation of many creatures; some ritual with celebration. I was in this palace before, it is very high in the sky, and there were no more clouds. I started checking if everything was all right, everything prepared. The white columns reached to the sky as if there was no ceiling. In the center, a wide marble staircase, with white steps, suddenly emerged, like a road, stretching into the distance – so far – you could not see what was downstairs. The staircase was very wide. On the sides, there were those who were waiting for the feast to begin.

I was checking two big silver trays standing on both sides – there were strange fruit on those trays[13] – like huge amber tangerines with their skin peeled away, without white particles, just little lines. But these were not tangerines, they were divine fruit. Without peel, shining through like amber – they were prepared, about ten on each tray. They were the most important items for the ritual. I started looking. While I was away to fight the monster – I could not understand how someone could commit a sacrilege – about three fruit were missing on each tray. But I was checking at the last moment, because the number of them was very

---

[13] All the way in the dream we were escorted by a guide, someone orange (later I said – of amber color), a tangerine without peel. His name was YAN, or ZWING, ZWIANG – hard to say in human language, just like some clanking sound. So this "tangerine" was possibly some Spirit, which was to be a gift to God as a sacrifice. But maybe it was just an ancient fruit, which doesn't exist anymore.

important. I knew clearly, that it was a dainty piece –
but not for humans. People were far away downstairs; I
went to them later, for I knew the fruit was for my
retinue.

There was a king in the palace. God was in the church,
but he was not there, and the manager was a priest.
The same as me. The symbol was a spirit, He would
have come to the feast, and I was a manager, the
executive. The other executives were around me. The
spirit would have come, or His thoughts, or His light....
I was the lady of the kingdom. There were some
creatures – not people – around me, very tall, of huge
stature. The tall-sized creatures were very different,
their essences were different, like the birds, the grass,
as if one would have a head of an Eagle, and the other
of a Snake. I knew that for some of them these dainty
pieces of orange fruit were important for magic, for
consecration, and maybe later they would have eaten
them.

The Bold Eagle on the picture on the wall has such a
beak; as if he has eaten my fruit... An eagle with its
sharp beak can pick, peel and swallow them up very
quickly.

In short, I noticed it, I checked the fruits that were left
and went downstairs to the people. But maybe, because
there were not enough of them, they were losing their
quality, and they did not have the same quality
together. So I gave both trays to the people around me.
Maybe they had eaten them. I went down the stairs.
Downward, the staircase opened wide, like in Rome's
amphitheatres, and at the open side there was a stormy
ocean. It was a sunny day. I was up on the columns,
talking – up there, where the stairs were coming
together with the upper colonnade like amphitheatre.
There were crowds of people downstairs. They all were

wearing strange clothes – ancient Roman togas, and fabrics fastened by a buckle on the shoulder, and in short iron skirts, in chain armor – all different designs. But there were no wild ones, everybody was normal. They were standing in the amphitheatre, and on the beach – but they were not swimming, not sunbathing. I was looking at the sea – the sea was important. It was stormy, I looked carefully – it was dangerous. It was boiling from something inside it. Some herds were coming out of it by groups – some elephants, and other creatures. They were not animals. I went down. When I found myself in some narrow corridor just before the amphitheatre, I saw that some new creatures began to appear from the ocean – they were some kind of deer, or rather goats – a huge mass, they were walking very closely to each other – horns, hooves, many hooves. And I understood, that it became dangerous – many hooves. They were coming one after another, you could not stop them. And then I told to my surrounding to leave. Actually, I was not talking – I had a sign. But in that corridor people were running towards me – they all were rushing to the ocean. I was telling them, that it is dangerous, "don't do it" – but they were running, and blocking my way and the way of my people up... I don't remember, what happened afterwards...

"So those goat-deer disturbed your celebration?"

Not at all. It is like if you prepare yourself for a feast, invite some guests, and then in a free moment, you go to the window to look outside – I was watching the scene from somewhere above it.

I saw this statue on the beach on the sand in Acumal, Riviera Maya, and it reminded me about this dream and this goat-deer, unusual animal with many hooves. Maybe they existed thousands of years ago?

Animals with hooves from the ocean

Dream # 14
I was Very Thin and Extremely Tall, February 11, 1997

In my dream you hold me. I was the size of a little baby, such a small size, fitting in your hands. But I am very, very tall... I see myself from the side. I am very thin, legs stretching far from the ground, wearing a white, transparent dress.... It was my real appearance, the way I looked at that time. I am with you; we are in the big hall somewhere far, far in the Universe. And there, different Spirits have gathered. It was an enormous huge hall, a ball-room. I am a tall, thin figure dressed in white. If I were a person, a human being, I would be probably three-meters tall or more which made me look even thinner than I was. And I did not have weight. Weight did not exist – it looked like we were only souls in that dream, at that moment.

However, this was not a dream. It was some kind of special, very real – another reality – a special condition. It felt as if I was going through deep water; if you try to talk, for example, it is very difficult. We went there from time to time. We know this place and what it is all about. I go there often while I am sleeping, in this strange condition. And *you* were in the middle of a hall. *You* held me. I was very, very light and very-very tall. I cannot see these *Spirits* directly. They speak about me, discuss my snow-white clothes. It was multilayered, made of the thinnest possible fabric, pure, shimmering fabric. I cannot hear what they say. They are all around me, looking at me and talking about me. I can see only myself from the side. It's a double sensation. The first sensation; I see you and me from the side, and at the same time, I feel myself in *your* hands and how I hold your neck, I even feel the softness of your skin.

This is all so real.... Then you left, and carried me out of that room and out of that space. I asked you, "What did they spoke about?" You told me that they spoke about my dress. Somehow, I was sleeping there. When I was there I felt everything, but I did not understand anything, nothing made sense. We came out and into another space. There I could understand and talk to you already, no more of that influence. We were in such a strange magic world!

****

The original Atlanteans were of extra-terrestrial origin and came to earth over 50 thousand years ago. They were of human shape, but not the modern earth humans as we are.

They were very tall and fair skinned* and probably originated from the Lyrian star system. They are also

76

known as the Elohim or Annunaki and their story is hidden in the texts of Genesis. They had life spans of around 800 years and are known in some texts as 'the tall ones'.

Dream # 15
ATHARVAN, October 13, 1989

In the morning, I remembered the word from yesterday – EQUINOX, I was repeating it yesterday all the time. It was there before my waking up, always like a drop of water pecking the stone. EQUINOX... EQUINOX... EQUINOX....

Now I have the same sensation. But this time the word is different. This was like a flow, repeating the same word.... It was only one minute. I woke up, looked toward the window and closed my eyes again. And at this moment (I felt a shiver on my skin); I immediately saw the face of a man of a huge size. Maybe it was an enormous statue. My field of view captured an eye, a cheek, the chin on the left side. I was so staggered, shaken, that it disappeared. Afterwards, it appeared again, and again – I am stunned – it disappeared.

It was the face of a man, made of grey marble. But there was a feeling that he was alive. On the side there was a pattern, something I saw on Chinese walls in China, and on his face there were many, many manuscripts of a very fine design. The face was of a single-color, and the pattern on the edge of the chin – a darker shade. The curvy writing was on the cheek in a triangle shape. He had Persian, almond-shaped eyes. And there was a word, which stuck with me, much harder than the word EQUINOX – it was repeating again and again ... constantly, rapidly. In my dream I thought that I would forget it, when I woke up. So I tried to remember. Maybe two words – avatar. And the word "vat" or "tar". I composed it from three words "vat", "tara". Something

that was repeating all the time – "avatar", and somewhere there was also the word, "hat".
A V A T A R A … A H A T A V A R A …- Atharvan, maybe?

Yes! Exactly that word! I think it was the word. It was this one, whose face I saw. But I could not bear it, only for a moment, then everything blurred, I could not bear to look for a long time. I was there for an instant – a few times. Just like a quantum of light[14] of grey-dim color. It was not a marble – marble shine. I could draw it, how it was, what proportions there were. The finest drawing, as if his face was the size of a room, but traced with exquisite precision. (I drew this picture immediately after I woke up. I never expected that it would be featured in a future book.) Was he sleeping? I don't remember. He radiated the sensation of a living being. And I did not feel that I was sleeping.

Atharvan

---

[14] You will find Scientific Interpretation about quantum light at the end of the book, "The Re-birth of an Atlantean Queen", by Julia SvadiHatra.

Atharvan (अथर्वन् *, atharvan-; an n-stem with nominative singular* अथर्वा *atharvā)*
Vedic atharvan is cognate with Avestan atharvan, "priest", but the etymology of the term is not yet conclusively established. (Boyce, 1982:16)

Dream # 16
Zarathustra in Water, September 6, 1993

It was a dream at night, but it was like a vision. I have a feeling that I was not sleeping. I was standing on the shore of a little round lake, near a high bluff. I was looking at the reflection in the water. The surface reflected a person of huge size. His reflection was on the surface, but it partially went under water, it was three-dimensional, and I could see him. I was conversing before that about astrology, or just contemplating. I wanted to see him. He was either high in the clouds or standing up on the hill. I thought that, in fact, he was in the clouds, but in order to make it seem real, he offered a conventional way, as if he was standing on the top of the hill and was reflected in the water, in order to calm my imagination down. *I knew that I could not; I was unable to look straight at him. But he wanted to show himself to me – at least as a reflection in the water. Maybe I saw my own reflection?*

Zoroaster (Latinized from Greek variants) or Zarathushtra (from Avestan Zaraθuštra), also referred to as Zartosht (Persian: زرتشت *), was an ancient Iranian prophet and religious poet. The hymns attributed to him, the Gathas, are at the liturgical core of Zoroastrianism.*

Dream # 17
Huge Woman on a Cupola-Sphere, January 31, 2005

We were sitting in a big house full of expensive things –
the rococo furniture, everything solid, rich – carpet etc.
There were my grandmothers, grandfathers, my
ancestors. I had a feeling, that it was my native home.
There was some symbol, a sign – either a sound, noise,
wind – some kind of fall-through. Something happened
to me, I began feeling something. And I went out. As a
result of this "something", I turned up in a desert, no
trees, no grass, no animals … And the voice said to me
that a miracle was found on Earth (like in Pushkin's
fairy-tales "divo") – a woman of huge size. I was moving
towards the north-west, turning northward. I saw her
immediately – on the right, to the north. There was a
mount on the right, like a hill, you could see a sphere, it
began at my feet and I was floating on its edge. And
there she was, on top of this big sphere, like on a
mounted hill, standing – a huge living woman, very nice,
friendly, close to nature, natural herself, like a peasant
woman. Very welcoming face, high cheekbones, like a
skinny, Indian. She had almond shaped eyes, plain,
clean national dress with beautiful embroidery, olive
color face and rosy cheeks, roundish nostrils. She had
very strong, enormous power. Not heavy, just the
opposite – tall and slim. I did not see anybody with my
eyes, but I felt that there were invisible creatures
surrounding her: up to her knees, up to her waist – they
were surrounding her, taking care of her. I saw her not
from the bottom-up, but as if contrariwise, since I saw
all of her – from the bottom – I would not have been able
to see all of her. I looked at her and admired her. I
returned home and told everyone, "Turn on the radio
and TV, such a woman has been found now!"

Dream # 18
A message from the Magnificent Maya people, June 24, 2008

I was up in the temple, standing near the entrance, and looked down. Everything was under the golden sunset light. I see the Temple of Warriors. Hundreds of warriors were standing on the bright red stairs. One by one, in total silence, all of them looking at me up here. Short skirts, belts, necklaces and spears reflected the sunset light.... I saw the sunlight going through their eyes. I saw their shiny black hair, toned legs and arms' muscles.... Columns made a long shadow....

I felt that my astrologers in the Caracol were also frozen in time.... I saw Maya people sitting on the ground around the pyramid with their children, wives and old parents.... These are all my people... I know each and everyone of them. I blessed them when they were born and when they were married. Many came to me for help when they were sick, or for support and advice. This is my Big Family.

I turned back and looked inside the temple. My old teacher, the Priest, is sitting with his tortoise in his hands. All my people were around me dressed in beautiful, colorful outfits with feathers, masks and shiny, luxurious jewelry. The Snake, the Eagle and Anubis were nearby as usual. They all looked at me very seriously – they were waiting in total silence. From the corner of my eye, I saw long, tall figures, watching all of us in the distance.

It felt as if TIME had stopped and they were all frozen in that moment.... All these people were cut and separated from us and our time....

Kukulcan

Something in between ... in between times ... and it was burning. I saw a big fire. I looked closely. It was literally mountains of ancient books and manuscripts burning in this fire! I saw some manuscripts that were very deep at the bottom of the dark ocean, that were covered with sand, near parts of a wooden *baroque*-styled ship.

Then I receive the message...

****

Now I will try to tell the message. I am not sure that people will be able to understand what this message means, especially since it was given to me in ancient Maya. I will try some simple modern way and in English – although English is not my native language....

As a High Priest of Chichen Itza from ancient Mayan people to each human been living on Earth: -

I am re-incarnated after thousands of years, maybe to give you a message in the special time of ending of 13-baktun cycle.

Chichen Itza is not just another tourist attraction.

This city is where my people, my family, my friends lived beautiful, bright, happy lives. People were creative and deeply spiritual. The ancient Mayan people who built Chichen Itza had highly developed culture, science, architecture, astronomy, most advance astrology and were in constant connection with God and with the parallel world in space.

We lived in great Harmony with the Energy of our Planet, Space, Sound, Plants, Animals, Rocks and Ocean. Some of us had the ability to travel in time and we accumulate the most valuable information as a precious gift to the human race. What people know now about ancient Maya Wisdom and Knowledge is just the tip of the iceberg.

Curse forever those Spanish conquistadors who tried to destroy all of our books and history which belonged to the next world's generations.

This information, this KNOWLEDGE exists and is available always to those who are really willing to study it.

Our life is not what you saw in the movie Apocalypse! It never had happened this way in Chichen Itza in my lifetime.
It is wrong how they portrayed us; we are noble, beautiful, kind-hearted people.

Misunderstanding or lack of knowledge about our culture and history is not the way to create something from your own mind, and turn it into public display trying to make money on the energy emanating from fear, blood and suffering. Shame on those who used our Holy pyramid for this purpose, and tried to cast a shadow on my pure temple in return.

They should fix this mistake to avoid karma punishment.

The Pyramid was always very special place for the meetings with God and Spirits.

It was a House of Souls. It was our Big, Perfect Crystal. It was my home and my place of work.

Kukulcan

Creativity is the only one important product on Earth and the reason for people to be here.

Those talented producers who will create a great movie about us in the next three years will receive our special blessing.

This Pyramid is an important part of our Galactic structure as an energy and information exchange between the Earth and the Cosmos. The Earth's energy flows through the underground configuration of the pyramid, from inside out with the help of her little twin-sister pyramid, which connected them on the top with the Cosmos energy of the Universe. This Pyramid is part of a chain, comprising other pyramids, forming one centre which accumulates enormous concentration of powerful energy, especially during Equinox time.

It will be nice to continue to perform rituals with a Priest in it, who will connect people with the God.
SNAKE, EAGLE, ANUBIS and JAGUAR energy should be present at special celebration time.

Soon will be the beginning of a new Katun and Baktun time cycles.

Difficult times of changes are starting now. Planet and world around overwhelmed by the side effect of huge population and in need of rest. Please stop expanding your family by bringing new spirits to the Earth for the next seven years. You will learn that it will help your family and you personally dramatically. Don't let outside fear take control over your inner voice and your own spirit. Stay in Harmony. We have many lives. Remember that your guardian angel is always near to support you.

Creativity and Love will help your Spirit be strong and survive the Time of Big Changes and proceed to the higher stage of evolution.

PRIEST JAGUAR, MAGICIAN.

Dream # 19
Luminous Bodies of Plants, January 8, 1992

I hadn't slept all night. Again, like the other times, I was dreaming of unusual things within five minutes of my being asleep. I can remember it, because I woke up right after that. It was maybe 5:00am. I was lying in bed. At this moment a terrible sound, a terrible click made me open my eyes – as if some shot went off in my room. I remembered my dream – and at the same moment, there was this shot, a terrible sound, like dry wood cracking. I jumped, opened my eyes, and I could still hear the shot. Something like that used to happen with my piano. I fell back to sleep and again something unusual came to my dreams. Again, this shot, and I woke up again. Very strong sound.

I was dreaming that I approached the window, there was some space in front of me, and different kinds of trees had been planted in rows. There were some apple trees, pines, birch-trees, a whole variety, and rare breeds as well. I looked at them. In my mind, I knew what kind of trees they were, but with my eyes, I saw them in colors. I was shocked – I hadn't seen this before. The trees of the same breed were of the same color. They had approximately three spectra. I remembered what apple trees looked like, their color was orange; what the fir trees looked like – they consisted of three lines of the spectrum, I think, bright blue. If the blue is responsible for dynamic of growth, it should be on the top, where the new growth is. But it turned out to be not so, the fir tree had it in the middle,

2/3 from the bottom – a blue line, then bright-yellow, and perhaps a red one. I don't remember now, I cannot remember clearly. The apple tree had a soft orange tone, coming into rose, but two separate colors, like on those balloons.

You opened a book and started reading – a prologue. You were reading aloud with my voice. At the same time, the other me, was observing the scene from outside. I interrupted your reading. I knew what was written there, right away, although I heard it for the first time. In this book, the knowledge came to the surface, which was unknown to people until then. This book was a revelation. People did not even suspect it – it opened up, revealing itself like an old secret, a treasure, as if someone dug it out of the earth. A very rare animal, a diamond animal was buried there thousands and thousands of years ago. I interrupted myself and started dictating the already specific things from this book (you had only the introduction). You started to write down what I was saying immediately.

Dream # 20
Ruby Emerald, February 11, 1988

I remember now the other thing…. There is a huge living space. I saw something like that in some Hollywood-shooting sets. And in this space, there is a ruby crystal, and she is standing on top – this woman…. It is like a cathedral and a hall with the wall which repeated the form of a crystal. There was an enormous big crystal in the middle of a circle. And this crystal was surrounded with a liquid, but this is not water. The walls are black (dark) inside; there is nothing there, not a thing, no entrance or exit. In the middle, there is a huge circle, surrounded by high molded, synthetic barrier (colloid), quite accurately placed. Inside, there is a cave with water, but it is not water, and on it, there is a

Bordeaux-red, huge, precious stone, floating, very bright, succulent. "Emerald" – the pronouncing of the word becomes this stone. Bright, cherry color. Deep, bright edges. The woman is standing on the top of the stone. I look from above, like a huge person. The woman is standing like little Thumbelina, dressed in white. The fabric of her dress runs down in waves, and it seems there is a shining pattern.... It is not water, not steam.... It is a pool filled with some substance. It is thick like quicksilver, light as steam, heavy – everything is covered with it, the pool is full, a lot of it. But the crystal is not covered, all its facets meet on top, and there is this beauty, the one that gave away the belt and the sheath, and she looks up, she aims from the top of her head, like a ray – up, everything in her is aiming just there. The strange substance around her, not water, it slightly reminds me of slime, when some energy was coiling around my arms, and something was humming, I remember now! I know – it was the product of those creatures. There was a lot of it then! I know this strange substance.... It is something in between, colloid.... It is one of the components....

Chapter 2

Kukulcan

Dream #21
Kukulcan (Human-Lizard), September 19, 1991.

The sky is the color of alexandrite, a violet gemstone. Everything around is yellow – it is clay. This clay consists of polyhedrons, which are stuck together, like graphite, stratified.

The time of day..., there was no sun, but it was very light, similar to a white night in the North Pole. He had the same violet eyes as the sky, with orange, round pupils. He looked like a lizard – a man-lizard. He was half-sitting.

He is green – the scales of cactus petals, but not prickly. Near the temples, the scales are small, then they become bigger and bigger and grow into a beautiful crest on his head. It looks very neat and precise. He did not react to me, so to speak. I saw it on myself first, beginning with the neck, and then I looked at him from all sides. At the beginning, I felt as if his skin was on me, and I began to transform into *it*.

He was very quiet. There was a feeling of deep, unknown mystery or wisdom, enveloping him, like an aura. The green emerald scales were covering his skin, which was glowing under them. Maybe the skin was bright orange. I think, yes, it was of a glowing, orange color. He looked like a well-designed, very detailed piece of jewelry, but real, and alive at the same time, which made him even more priceless. We were near each other for some time. I don't recollect now what happened afterwards.

I woke up and looked at the clock near my bed. The day was 19.09.1991. The memory of him stayed with me for maybe a month until I began to see him again and again. I saw him about 8 to 10 times during that year. He is a "really cool guy", adorable in his perfection. He is like a beautiful, rare toy with an electronic mechanism inside him. I describe him as having "electronic insides", perhaps because he seems so advanced and modern to me.

****

Now, 17 years later, suddenly this particular hairstyle, with a crest, is in fashion for boys. Every time I see a boy with such a hairstyle, it reminds me of my lizard friend. I then decided to draw him, to show you what I mean or to remind myself how he looked at the time I had that first dream of him.

When I was looking for a pencil, I came across some advertising pamphlet that said, *"The future is friendly."* (TELUS © all rights reserved) This is good news, by the way!

While I was drawing him I began to think that it is possible that I like him because he is green, the color of plants and his scales are like cactus leaves, which gives him this rare human and plant look. My dream has come true! I always wished to be as close as possible to plants – and he is two-in-one, both plant and human at the same time. I wish I could be like him!

Once I was envious, when I saw in a magazine someone's kitchen in Mexico with a real tree growing through the house! Imagine that! You could sit all day long, your body leaning against a real live tree, and type on your computer!

Kukulcan

Well..., I sketched him very fast and here he is. I didn't draw the small scales on his face – you can add them with your imagination.

Kukulcan

He has a human face, not a lizard or reptile kind of face. He has a small nose and lips ... and long narrow eyes.

When I began paying attention to this, I made an astonishing discovery! First, boys and girls with this "punk" hairstyle may have seen these kinds of people in their dreams! They don't remember the dreams but they wish to adopt this hair style, perhaps because they feel comfortable with it, or their hair to be shaped in such a fashion is appealing to them. Similar to what I am feeling when I wear my jaguar jacket. The same is probably true of those modern people who have their whole body covered with tattoos. Maybe, in their past lives, they lived in some culture where people had tattoos on their bodies from a young age, and that's the way they used to see themselves – somewhere in Africa, or Australia or India....

Since the unusual developments that have occurred during the last five months of my life, I began seeing people in a different way. I began understanding them and being more tolerant of their choices in life. People who look weird in our eyes, all these punks, tattooed bodies, who wear strange outfits – maybe their preference with this strange, weird style comes from their past lives through their dreams.

Roman Gladiator's helmet

91

When I traveled through Italy this summer, near the Coliseum, in Rome, I saw men in gladiators' outfits. They too, had the same kind of plumage shape on their helmets. I found the same thing in Greece!

I am telling this because it happened to me and, in my life, I started adopting behaviors or following styles which I saw in my dream; it started to be part of my lifestyle.

But let's go back to this sentence: *"When I began paying attention to this, I made an astonishing discovery!"* I started paying attention to the SHAPE of the head.

The hairdressers in Chichen Itza shaped my hair in this style. They lifted my hair up and turned it towards the front of my head. They made a ponytail at the end; sometimes they divided and made two ponytails. One day they cut some of my hair because it was getting too long and I saw myself in profile – I looked exactly the way I did in my dream. The whole of my hair had been pulled to the front and lifted into a ponytail – very nice indeed.

****

It is the next day right now, in the morning. I just woke up. 6:00 a.m. A heavenly, enchanting fragrance surrounds me, from the white lily near my bed.... I am lying down in bed thinking about this unusual head-shape I drew yesterday. For some reason, I felt there was something important about it...

I start remembering... and now I am at my desk, typing....

Yesterday evening, it was very warm on English Bay. It was Saturday. There were lots of people on the beach. I regret not to have taken my camera with me, because there were many boys around with this hairstyle, more than I ever saw in one place at one time! And there are millions of them all over the World! Some have their hair shaped in a high crest, others in smaller styles. There are all kinds of variety of this crested hairdo! But if they let their hair grow a little bit longer, it will be shaped as my lizard friend had.

Then I remembered the statue of the Lord King Pakal I saw at the hotel in Cancun, he had his hair shaped in the same fashion!

Lord King Pakal

Next, I remembered things that are even much more important!

This headdress or style is exactly the same as the shaped hats the Buddhists, the Egyptians, and the

Kukulcan

Mexican priests wore! All of them, all over the world wear this shape of helmet, hat or hairstyle!

My aunt Merry told me that when I was a little girl I loved a woolen hat with a little ball in front. I even wanted to sleep with it on. Then I started paying attention to what she said. The shape of this baby hat was exactly the same as the hairstyle worn by this "priest".

Julia: the "Little Priest"

Later, on the same day, I was sitting on my favorite bench in the rose garden in Stanley Park. I was drawing the Buddhists' hats. Well..., it is not really comfortable to draw with your sketch book in your lap, but you have the idea of what I am talking about.

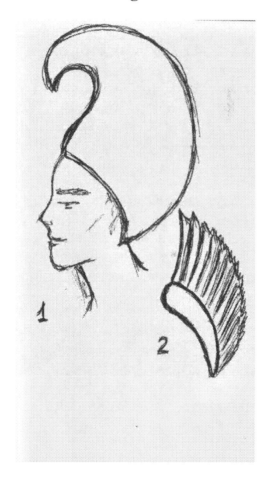

1: International Priests hat shape
2: Buddhist hat

O my God!
God...???

Kukulcan

When, I searched *"god with scales"* on one smart website:
http://www.crystalinks.com/god with scales, here's what came out!!!
God with scales, here's what came out!!!

One entity played key roles as creator in Atlantis, Egypt, Sumer, India among other myths about creation. In Mesoamerica and Peru he was known as Quetzalcoatl, among other roles he played. His pyramid was the Pyramid of the Sun in Teotihuacán Quetzalcoatl ("feathered snake") is the Aztec name for the Feathered-Serpent deity of ancient Mesoamerica, one of the main gods of many Mexican and northern Central American civilizations.

The name "Quetzalcoatl" literally means quetzal-bird snake or serpent with feathers of the Quetzal (which implies something divine or precious) in the Nahuatl language. The meaning of his local name in other Mesoamerican languages is similar. The Maya knew him as Kukulkán; the Quiché as Gukumatz.

The Feathered Serpent deity was important in art and religion in most of Mesoamerica for close to 2,000 years, from the Pre-Classic era until the Spanish Conquest. Civilizations worshiping the Feathered Serpent included the Olmec, the Mixtec, the Toltec, the Aztec, and the Maya. http://www.crystalinks.com/quetzalcoatl.html

He was known as the inventor of books and the calendar, the giver of maize corn to mankind, and sometimes as a symbol of death and resurrection. Quetzalcoatl was also the patron of the priests and the title of the Aztec high priest.

Next I found:

Snake-bird gods fascinated both Aztecs and pharaohs, By Robin Emmott.

Ancient Mexicans and Egyptians who never met and lived centuries and thousands of miles apart both worshiped feathered-serpent deities, built pyramids and developed a 365-day calendar, a new exhibition shows." There are huge cultural parallels between ancient Egypt and Mexico in religion, astronomy, architecture and the arts. The exhibition, which opened at the weekend in the northern Mexican city of Monterrey, shows how Mexican civilizations worshiped the feathered snake god Quetzalcoatl from about 1,200 BC to 1521, when the Spanish conquered the Aztecs. From 3,000 BC onward Egyptians often portrayed their gods, including the goddess of the pharaohs Isis, in art and sculpture as serpents with wings or feathers. MONTERREY, Mexico, Sept 24 (Reuters Life!) -

The Sumerian God also has the same "hair style" as the one I saw on my man-lizard! Wow! I am impressed; this is additional proof that I saw the real Kukulcan in my dreams!

Flying (or "Bird") God and Sumerian God, Ashur
"The Sumerian Gods Created a Biogenetic Experiment
Called Humans"

What's more, the Sumerian God has wings – symbol of his ability to fly... and by the way, again, on their images, both of them carry water buckets.
http://www.crystalinks.com/sumergods.html

Below, he looks similar to my beautiful green human-lizard. Except mine has a human face. Also, below there is a photo of his pyramid – strange shape, it reminds me of something like a third of those sphere-shaped palaces, which I saw many times in my dreams

Quetzalcoatl   *Bas-relief from Chichen Itza*

Quetzalcoatl pyramid

After that, I read this sentence:

"The feathered serpent and the serpent alongside a deity signifies the duality of human existence, at once in touch with water and earth, the serpent, and the heavens, the feathers of a bird," said Ulloa.
http://africa.reuters.com/wire/news/usnN24278139.html

Don't you think it sounds too complicated?
I think in reality it is much easier.

Here is what this is really about...

It is my dear, green Lizard-Human visiting Mexico and other countries in the past, and people made him God. He has scales, so they call him lizard or snake. He arrived on Earth in some "flying object", so they also started adding bird qualities, such as feathers to his representation, wings that would give him the ability to fly. They called him "Quetzalcoatl", using two words together: bird-snake and serpent with feathers. *(The name "Quetzalcoatl" literally means quetzal-bird snake or serpent with feathers of the Quetzal.)* This is it! Nothing more.

Note: The original writings and drawings of this dream and all other dreams exist. At the time I had this dream, in 1991, I had no idea who this snake-bird-person was. I didn't have any idea that I would see "him" in Mexico just 6 months ago!

I repeat again here:
It is impossible for me to say that these dreams are from the Past or from the Future. Maybe what I saw there existed in the Past but still exists in the Present and will be in the Future.

I see it like a spooled thread, rolling one over the other and the other, and each of them is a span of time. Spooling the thread of ages in this manner explains that they are very close to each other, and running parallel to one another in space. At the same time, if a wormhole is formed amid the threads of this bobbin, it can be easily understood how people, ships, trains, animals disappeared in one place, only to re-appear in a different place at a different time – traveling from one time to another.

The technology used in Atlantis was much more advanced than what we have now. Therefore, there is a strong possibility that I will begin remembering my past in dreams.

A New Mexican Membreno Apache chief told me recently that at certain times in human history, the past and the present snap back together as if they were two ends of a gigantic rubber band. He told me, "The past is now." The Hopi and Mayan origin stories, as well as those of the Incas, Aztecs, Caddos, O'odhams, and many other Indian tribes are at last telling us that all humans are interrelated. For me, that is a comforting thought in a world that has been fragmenting almost beyond redemption (Can Humpty Dumpty be put back together again? Gene D. Matlock © Copyright 2005).

Ouroboros is an ancient alchemy symbol depicting a snake or dragon swallowing its own tail, constantly creating itself and forming a circle. It is the Wheel of Time - The Alchemy Wheel – 12 around 1 to manifest grid programs that give the illusion of linear time allowing souls to experience emotions. Ouroboros is associated with Alchemy, Gnosticism and Hermeticism. It represents the cyclical nature of things, eternal return, and other things perceived as cycles that begin anew as soon as they end. In some representations the serpent is shown as half light and half dark, echoing symbols such as the Yin Yang which illustrates the dual nature of all things, but more importantly that these opposites are not in conflict.

Origins of the Ouroboros:
The serpent or dragon eating its own tail has survived from antiquity and can be traced back to Ancient Egypt, circa 1600 BCE. Crystallink.

Snake eating tail, Ouroboros

From another point of view, I was a Mexican Priest in Chichen Itza. According to Gene Matlock, during my past life as a Priest, I could meet people from the past and future in real life, travel through the Universe and perhaps visit Egypt and other places with their help. This is why I saw the Egyptian Anubis during the sacrifice ceremony on the top of the pyramid in the temple, and one man was there wearing an Egyptian hat, like that of the Nefertiti statues.

As with all Myths about Gods and Goddesses, Mayan creational mythology discusses connections with being from other realms that came to Earth to seed the planet. Many people connect the story of the Popol Vuh with a story of extraterrestrial Gods who came to earth and made man in their own image. When they first created man, he was perfect, living as long as the gods and having all of their abilities. Fearing their 'creation', the gods destroyed them. In the next evolution, a lower form of entity was created, 'human', as he exists today. Within Mayan culture they have legends of visiting Gods from outer space. As in all creational myths, religions, and prophecies, the gods promise to return one day (Maya Gods and Goddesses, CRYSTALINKS).

In Chichen Itza, the God KUKULCAN, looks like a man inside the jaw of a snake or serpent, on the sculpture of a bas-relief – the God Kukulcan is inside a flying snake. I tried to take a photo of the bas-relief, which is located in the Warrior temple, but it was far away. The picture did not come out well enough to be printed. However, I just found the same in India – God inside the snake's jaw!

God inside the snake's jaw, India

Snakes, God

Snake, India

What about this flying serpent? I mean this airplane which looks like a snake?
With whom, (me as a Priest) did I have contact in that Dream # 13 – The Upper Kingdom, October 24, 1993?

Well, I have some ideas about it.

I brought my creatures to this THING. Then something crawled out to meet me. It had green spots all over his white body. The wise one. It appeared, suspended in front of me. It was speaking with a soft voice, like Kaa (the huge snake in the cartoon about the Indian boy, Maugli). It said to me, "I will save yours, the little ones." And it began to unwind, unroll, as if it was crawling out of an invisible crack in the wall. There was an opening and it crawled out – I didn't see the inside of the place. It was growing in size – expanding, and became as big as a Hercules plane. From the tail a huge crack opened across its body leading my creatures inside it. Its head was flat, like a leaf. The crack was in the lower side – and my creatures started walking inside IT.

It is always a question for me, *Who* or *What* is this THING?

First, I know there is a legend in India, describing the civilization of Nag, which existed a long time ago. Nagy is a snake which is highly intelligent. Many temples in India have a snake represented in their construction – sometimes many heads are sculpted together. Even the steps on the temples – like those in Chichen Itza – have snakes statues on both sides at the foot of the stairs. Maybe it was some kind of real live creatures that existed in ancient times – some kind of intelligent, huge snake, a descendant of the dinosaur's family.

Lockheed – Airplane's entrance

Rudyard Kipling, Rikki-Tikki-Tavi
"Who is Nag?" said he. "I am Nag. The great God Brahm put his mark upon all our people, when the first cobra spread his hood to keep the sun off Brahm as he slept. Look, and be afraid!" He spread out his hood more than ever, and Rikki-tikki saw the spectacle-mark on the back of it that looks exactly like the eye part of a hook-and-eye fastening.

Let's go back to my dream. The entrance to this THING reminded me instantly of this snake's jaw, near the pyramid stairs in Chichen Itza and that of an airplane. I took a photo when I was there. This cost me a lot, by the way!

The first photo I took in Chichen Itza was at 8:00 a.m. I tried to take a shot of the snake's face – directly in front of it, but the rope was in my way, so I stepped over the rope.... As soon as I did, a guard ran up to me and brought me into the office where I was told that I wouldn't be allowed to visit the ruins for a full day – what a punishment!

Snake's jaw, Chichen Itza

Egypt – Temple of Abydos

http://www.ovnis.tv/noticias/2009/mayo/06mayII/cient_ruso.html

http://www.geocities.com/dominorus/atlantis.html

Just a month after I had the dream with my human-lizard I had another dream, in which I saw an airplane or starship entirely covered with scales, similar to snake scales.

Kukulcan

Dream # 22
Starship with Fish Scales, October 21, 1991

2 dreams in one night

Dream #1:

There was a church. Everyone was dressed in an old-fashion way. I turned up in this church on previous occasions.

There were two great-grandmothers. Everything was going on properly. Something happened in the church, I don't remember what. I was talking to my great-grandmothers – they were very attentive and polite. They were well dressed. Later on, I unexpectedly collapsed to the ground but something pulled me out of my trance immediately. And I turned up in a cosmic ship instantly. It was high – no gravity. The ship was the shape of a fish inside, narrowing at the ends; the floor was transparent, as if we were inside a bottle. It was important that there were no cracks and cavities, because it affected the ship's movement. The inside shape was also connected with its movement. Ahead there were two figures – with their backs to us. They wore silvery hoods which were sparkling with silver lights – threads. The Guide was with me, he was showing me all this. We were doing something together – I don't remember what. And these two – the silvery ones – floated to us and we communicated. The walls of the ship were like those of a chamber where they test sound transmissions, and something – hard to explain what – was protruding from the walls. These silvery ones were smaller than me, about 130 cm high. They were all covered with big fish scales. And something protruded from him – the size of a palm. It was covered with fish scales as well.

The two silvery ones were ahead of me – about 30 meters from me. Behind me there was a round door – the size of a big multistory building, like a huge barn. But everything was closed very tightly – no cracks. In front there was a silvery screen, a background for them. The screen was about 5 or 6 meters high, and if there was a plate, it encircled it, at the side of a wing. The floor was transparent and under it – a divergent surface with a scale. They didn't wear a helmet, but something like cotton wool, fine cotton, or "energy", which resembled a halo over the saints' heads on icons... I think I have an idea now who is on the icons.

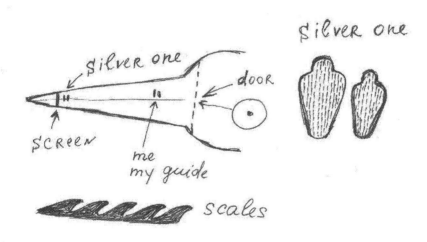

Drawing with the fish-scale airplane

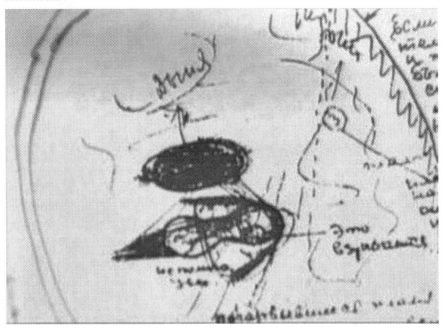

This is a picture, which was drawn by a Russian cosmonaut after he saw a strange object in space. There are similarities with the bottle shape, fish scales and so on, of my drawing. The only difference, in my dream, was that I was inside of it with my Guide and could only see part of it, without the engine part on the opposite side. [39]
http://www.veoh.com/videos/v554944aTQShtQA?g=cc
cp&rank=13&order=ca

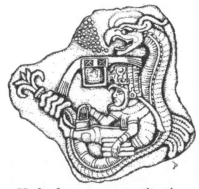

Kukulcan reconstitution

By the way, I mentioned before that monks travel in space often, this is their daily routine, so they meet these Spirits from the past or the future often.
Here is one of the drawings made by a monk.

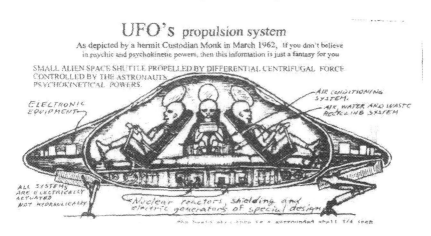

A monk's drawing

Another dream

Dream # 2
Diamond chain armor

I had some dresses, beautiful – about 20 or 30 of them made of fine fabric, with embroidery, excellent. I lived in a room, where I was putting on these dresses. There were mirrors, and the dresses were hanging around.

Later on, I went shopping with my grandmother. She told the sales lady that she ordered for me – I don't remember the word – something like a corset. It was made of fish scales, similar to a chain armor, which is only covering the upper part of the body, not the legs or arms. The whole thing was made in one piece – no seams. It was made of something so impressive that they all gasped – they could not imagine such a thing. And it was incredibly expensive, as if they were diamonds put together. I did not see the face and figure of my grandmother ... maybe she was my other grandmother.

****

First, the three dreams about "scales" repeated themselves in a one month interval. I already noticed this kind of pattern before. For example, for a few months, I had dreams about crystals and palaces mostly, afterwards I dreamt only of space travels, or only about plants...

Secondly, I collect dresses and tops which are made, in parts, of material that resembles fish scales and I look like a fish or snake in them. People, young and old alike, call me a "mermaid" when I am wearing this particular dress, because I have long blond hair and it makes the set complete. I love this dress. It is also interesting to note that I was attracted to shells, which look like scales. I was working with black pearls for some time. In one photo, I stand near black pearl shells, which look like scales!

Standing beside black pearl shells

Dress that looks like silver scales

In this next photo, I am sitting on a silver suitcase, I am wearing the silver dress, and silver shoes ... everything is just silver. This is what I mean when I say that people may develop strong habits from their dreams.

Silver scale dress, shoes and silver suitcases

Now it looks like everything is in great harmony with my clothes, because, finally, I have an explanation as to WHY things are the way they are.

I have some jaguar outfits, all kinds of jaguar shoes, bags, and gloves, etc. And now scales: diamond scales, silver outfits, silver bags and suitcases, silver-scale dresses, silver shoes, silver skirts, silver jackets, pens... Throughout my life, I just felt comfortable in these kinds of clothes, not just when they're in fashion.

Kukulcan

One company already has started making a documentary movie about all this and the evolution stemming from my past lives. I guess I should invite them to my home and they would see, with their own eyes, this collection of clothes – all related to my past.

The part below is not really important to read, you can easily skip it until you reach the middle: "WHO is this lizard, reptile?" Because suddenly the Priest woke up in me again and started to be a little bit angry and screamed: *"PLEASE leave our HOLY GOD, GOD of my Maya people, the great KUKULCAN, alone!"*

****

I started checking the internet and there are lots of theories. I found a book about ancient reptiles, which arrived on Earth and our civilization would have been issued from them.

Many authors, for example, researched this topic and proved this "start" and development up to our present time. They demonstrated that these reptiles, in many cultures, represented the face of God. YES, I agree. Very good! It is possible that my amazing friend, the human-lizard, is in fact, a KUKULCAN!

Maybe, a long time ago they came to Earth and helped people with their knowledge? And this is why the Maya people were so advanced and smart – same with the Egyptians and other cultures. BUT the next phase, according to some authors, is all wrong! Some of these authors were totally lost in this subject and tried to create confusion for the rest of the people. They started instilling fear and hate towards lizards, reptiles in people's minds. Why? This is the symbol of Goddesses and pride in all religions and culture, for some solid reason. These authors simply did not respect the most spiritual part, which people hold sacred in their hearts, the most precious love on the planet – the Love of God! There are hundreds of millions, maybe a few billions of people on Earth who live in Eastern Asia: India, China, Korea, Thailand and so on, who have anything but reverence and respect for the "Snake".

What are these authors doing? They try to cut people from their foundation, their roots, and their religion, which connects them and keeps all of them strong together. As a result, it could make them spiritually weak and easily manipulated. And, most importantly, the reptilian gene connection with people has not been proven in their theory. So "Show me the money!" Please bring me one drop of human blood, saliva, one hair, anything... where lizard genes are mixed with the human genes. It does not exist. I had in my own hands a live chick with human hair on it, 20 years ago. A few years ago, I saw a potato plant which "grew" chicken eggs instead of potatoes!

I know this kind of genetic research first hand... If it was done thousands of years ago, at least one sample would come out. Or a few people with lizard's scales would be born. Maybe they mean something else, some invisible connection? Possible. But no matter what, all this should not affect the ancient Goddess's symbols. So..."PLEASE *leave our HOLY GOD, GOD of my Maya people, the great KUKULCAN, alone!"*

Now, I will tell everyone some truths.

WHO is this human-lizard in my dream?

Below are some excerpts from a book entitled, "Globe Teaching", about astrological predictions in 1990, which I published under the pen-name "Magician" – which I know now as the High Priest of Chichen Itza.

In this book, predictions come independently from each other. These people lived sometimes 300 to 500 years apart – no phone, internet or fax. According to the predictions of Ranio Nero, Nostradamus, Edgar Cayce and many other astrologers and prophets, climate will dramatically change on Earth. The human skin will start changing; it will start to have spots at first, and afterwards, it will start growing some form of scales to protect the skin. And our color will also change. According to Nostradamus, people will have green scales! Another author (who will remain nameless) was saying that no one knows what Nostradamus tried to say by that.... Maybe we should not take this remark at face value, maybe he meant something else.... However, I know for a fact that Nostradamus wrote exactly what he meant. I saw people with green scales.

I have had other dreams with different kinds of people from the future. They had grey and lilac skin, lilac eyes, and their hair and nails were green. Maybe later, these extremities will develop into green scales.

People's vision will also change, according to these predictions. Many people will lose their vision. Some will start growing a membrane to cover and protect their eyes like reptiles have. Nostradamus and Ranio Nero said the same: "When people will see the second Sun and the second Moon their eyes will be closed." It means that they will be blinded by the strong radiation and light. I am sure you all know about this second Sun and Moon.

Back to the green color. Maybe it will be because people will start producing chlorophyll such as plants produce, with some genetics help, or our body will start to do this without help, and, this way, they will create extra oxygen? Maybe there will be too much carbon dioxide in the air?

What I am trying to convey here is that this human-lizard with scales on top of the skin is only a representation of what we will become, ourselves, in the future. Nothing more. It's that simple.

This human with lizard scales is possibly the God Kukulcan. He is a really cool and brave guy!

He is the one who survived and went through the generations and rows of transformations to attain ultimately this scaly cover, which protects him from a harmful environment. He is like a hero, like a warrior.

Maya warrior

Kukulcan

Warrior? Wow, I just remembered that I saw one like him – another statue in a hotel in Tulum.

By the way, did you see round white huge earrings on him? The first time I saw it during my past life hypnosis session about Chichen Itza, I laughed that all men, and nobles alike, would be wearing this kind of button-like earrings! Now I know exactly why they wore these earrings!

God Kukulcan, who looked like a man lizard, had these round circles about his ears such as all iguanas have! Since the Maya nobles and warriors were copying Kukulcan, they also copied these round circles at the side of its head and wore these white button-like earrings!

Giant iguana with white button-like "earrings"

On the Mexican road signs referring to "Iguanas Crossing" in Mexico.
You can also see this round circle on its head!

NOW WHO IS THIS TALL LONG FIGURE IN MY DREAMS? And why do people build pyramids?

Those who are way too big, the size of huge statues? I started searching, trying to find answers for myself first of all.

It was interesting that while I was writing this book, I actually studied myself through the puzzles of my dreams and hypnosis sessions, with the help of scientific research. I found a lot of answers and now it turns into pictures and each and everyone piece fits into the puzzle nicely together. I still have some "unsolved mystery", but it makes me happy and optimistic that I have the material to work with to continue my search further.

Dream # 13 – The Upper Kingdom, October 24, 1993

There was a king in the palace. God was in the church, but he was not there, and the manager was a priest. The same with me. The symbol was a spirit; He would have come to the feast, and I am a manager, the executive. The spirit would have come, or His thoughts, or His light.... I am the lady of the kingdom. There were some creatures – not people – around me, very tall, of huge size. The tall-sized creatures were very different, their essences were different, like the birds, the grass, as if one would have a head of an Eagle, and the other of a Snake.

Now see Dream #18 - A message from the Magnificent Maya people, June 24, 2008

I turned back and looked inside the temple. My old teacher, the Priest, is sitting with his tortoise in his hands. All my people were around me dressed in beautiful, colorful outfits with feathers, masks and shiny, luxurious jewelry. The Snake, the Eagle and Anubis were nearby as usual. They all looked at me very seriously – they were waiting in total silence. From the corner of my eye, I saw long, tall figures, watching all of us in the distance.

And again these enormous, tall people in the dreams: # 15 Atharvan, October 13, 1989; Zaratustra in Water, dream # 16, September 6, 1993; Huge Woman On A Cupola-Sphere, dream # 17, January 31, 2005; dream # 20, Ruby Emerald, February 11, 1988

I saw this giant, this enormous-size man near me, sitting in front of a pyramid. He bent one arm and turned toward me. Then I saw his blue eyes, so close that I even saw his breath... I even saw the wrinkles around his eyes –

everything in all of the little details. I could not sleep after that.... I was deeply shocked and it would be difficult for me to describe the sensation I experienced.

Instantly I saw the face of a huge woman looking at me through the window, she was so big, that she needed to bend to see me through the window. Her face covered almost half of the window of my bedroom! It was so sudden that I yelled, "Oh!!!" So my daughter ran into the room and asked, "What happened?" My daughter stayed near my bed. I closed my eyes and continued to see this big woman! She was at least 7 to 8 meters tall or taller – I guess – because we live on the third floor!

Why do such enormous-size statues exist in Egypt?

This summer, I saw in the Cairo museum and in the Louvre in Paris King Akhenaton with his daughter who all had enormous, long scalps, including Nefertiti, his wife. By the way the name Nefertiti, obviously comes from the word Neferu. When I asked a worker in the Cairo museum why the king and his daughter had such an unusual skull, he replied that maybe they were aliens....

By the way in dream #15 Atharvan, Zarathustra in Water; dream #16, Huge Woman On A Cupola-Sphere; dream # 17, Kukulcan; and in dream # 21, they are all with Persian-alien-almond shaped eyes, like on the next photo of the giant Neferu.

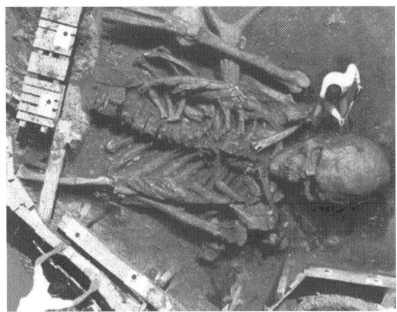

A giant in the "Empty Quarter"
with the Neferu-shaped eyes

Recent exploration activity in the Northern region of India uncovered the skeletal remains of a human of phenomenal size. This region of the Indian desert is called the Empty Quarter. See the photo and note the size of the two men standing in the picture in comparison to the size of the skeleton!! A very small article on this was published in Times of India - Mumbai edition on 22-Apr-2004.

The discovery was made by National Geographic Team (India Division). The Government of India has secured the whole area and no one is, allowed to enter except the NatGeo personnel.
http://padmasrinivas.blogspot.com/2007/05/bhimas-son-gadotkach-like-skeleton.html

Another huger skeleton here:

Also, a GIANT NEPHILIM OF SIZE 170 FEET found. It was exposed as a result of devastation tsunami in Thailand. 170 feet is about 50 meters – the same size as Nefellium's statue near the city of Bamian in Afghanistan. *"Near this city there are five colossal statues of people from five previous races. The biggest one is a 52-meter man from the first Ephemera race. The sculpture is wrapped in a blanket that may indicate or symbolize its once fragile form."*
http://www.youtube.com/watch?v=n2k7cigzi6Y&NR=1

I found a very clear answer to all of this with the very interesting research done by Dr Valery Uvarov, Earth's Hidden Twin And The Birth Of Civilization (Nexus magazine, #15 Vol.5).[36]

Let us go back 15,000 years, to the historical period that the ancient Egyptian texts call "the First Time" (Zep

Tepi) or the era of the Neferu, "when the Neferu lived on the Earth and talked with people". The word Neferu (Netheru), translated as "gods", has a complex internal structure. The descriptions of the Neferu in the texts indicate that they were human beings with god-like abilities. It was these beings who gave people knowledge of mathematics, architecture, astronomy and medicine, of the structure of the solar system, of cyclical processes and the principles lying at the foundation of the universe. All that made Egypt great was received in its time from the Neferu. It would seem that the Neferu of the ancient Egyptians and the Nephilim of the Sumerians are travelers from another planet.

Now let's follow the most important parts of this brilliant article.

Now, let us move across to the Mesopotamian region, to the land of the Sumerians (the territory of present-day Iraq and Syria). This is not a random move: there, too, people built pyramidal edifices—the stepped ziggurats. The surviving written texts and legends of the ancient Sumerians also contain many mentions of some highly developed civilizations that "descended to Earth from the heavens" and collaborated closely with the elite of Sumer. The interaction between "gods" and humans became so close that a number of ancient texts speak openly of the "gods" having sexual relations with "earthly maidens". The result was the birth of children with unusual genetic abilities, described in legends as "demigods", who went on to become rulers of the land of Sumer. There is no counting the scientific achievements and technical innovations of the Sumerians, who devoted particular attention to the study of the sky and heavenly bodies, as well as of the Nephilim, the gods that "descended to Earth from the heavens".

Is such a thing possible? It's hard to believe; harder still to consider the logical consequences. After all, in school and in higher education our teachers gave, and are still giving, a completely different version of history. But if it is so, where exactly did these Neferu come from? Do the Egyptian writings contain at least some mention, some hint, that would throw light on this? Yes, there is something!

Revelations from the Egyptian *Book of the Earth.* Let's return to Egypt, to the Valley of the Kings. We are going to visit the tomb of Ramses VI, a pharaoh of the 20th dynasty during the New Kingdom period. We go inside to the upper level J, to the central part of the right hand wall. It is a fragment from the *Book of the Earth*, Part A, Scene 7. This image contains several layers of information, but we shall concentrate for the moment on the main thing. The figure in the centre of the composition is covered with yellow paint. Semen is dripping from his phallus onto the head of the little human figure. What associations does that bring to your mind? Egyptologists thought the same.

The figure in the centre is the Sun, hence the golden yellow color of his body. The phallus and semen allude to the giving of life! Look again. Running through the centre of the figure is a curved line. That's an orbit. It passes through the third chakra (the solar plexus), which is a direct indication of the position of the orbit. *Two* planets are shown on this orbit: one in front of the figure, the other behind. This composition plainly states that on the orbit of the Earth (the third out from the Sun) *two* planets are moving: the Earth and some other body. The Sun looks at the Earth, the size (mass) of which is less than the size of the planet behind the Sun's back. It is located diametrically opposite us, behind the Sun, so we cannot see it!

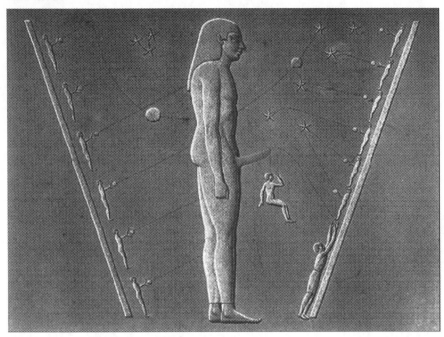

As for me, I am sure the Egyptians drew this man not only as a symbol of the Sun, but a man from Neferu. Egyptians drew him with exactly the same body size proportions as compared to normal size humans. Right near him they drew an ordinary human.

These discoveries of the giant skeletons support absolutely what I have been saying: these real giant skeletons on the previous photos with two people near them were exactly of the same proportions between the size of the giant from Neferu and the ordinary person near him. This was drawn on the wall of the *tomb of Ramses VI – fragment from the Book of the Earth, Part A, Scene 7.* The existence of this huge giant solves the mystery, which archeologists still have not explained to date: how it can be possible that different ancient structures on Earth have enormous weight and large size blocks with which they were built?

Everything depicted here is explained in brilliantly concrete fashion. The figure in the centre is the Sun, hence the golden yellow color of his body. The phallus and semen allude to the giving of life! Look again. Running through the centre of the figure is a curved line. That's an orbit. It passes through the third chakra (the solar plexus), which is a direct indication of the position of the orbit. *Two* planets are shown on this orbit: one in front of the figure, the other behind. This composition plainly states that on the orbit of the Earth (the third out from the Sun) *two* planets are moving: the Earth and some other body. The Sun looks at the Earth, the size (mass) of which is less than the size of the planet behind the Sun's back. It is located diametrically opposite us, behind the Sun, so we cannot see it! The distance from Earth to the Counter-Earth is so great that, bearing in mind the size of the Sun and the effects it produces; a fairly large heavenly body can be lost in the space behind the Sun....

Evidently, the Egyptians were seeking to set down for perpetuity information obtained from the Neferu. It therefore survived not only on the walls of tombs in the Valley of the Kings, but also in the cosmogony of the Pythagorean Philolaus who asserted, too, that behind the Sun (which he called Hestia, the central hearth) there was a body similar to our own planet—the Counter-Earth, or Anti-Earth."

The crescent body showing from behind the Sun is the 12th planet, which was lacking for an elegant and stable picture of the structure of the solar system that would accord with, among other things, the ancient texts. The Sumerians, incidentally, claimed that it was from the 12th planet of the solar system that "the Gods of Sky and Earth" descended to Earth."

Kukulcan

Next, in the article the author wrote that astronomers saw this Twin planet numerous times. The interesting part follows below, in which the secrets of this Counter-Earth seem well guarded by an invisible hand!

"A total of 140 X-ray images of the Sun were relayed to Earth, and if Phobos 1 had continued photographing then it would have taken a shot leading to an historic discovery. But in 1988, that discovery was not supposed to happen, so the world's news agencies reported that contact with Phobos 1 had been lost. The fate of Phobos 2, launched on 12 July 1988, was similar. The last picture that Phobos 2 sent back to Earth showed a huge, cigar-shaped, elliptical object that evidently deflected the probe."

Well..., it looks like the Neferu still exist out there and prefer to continue to be invisible and keep their secret deep from us. Such a turn of events is admittedly rather puzzling – but then, gradually, everything begins to fit into place. Therefore, the first conclusion from what has been stated, which we shall set in a prominent place, is that the "source" of the ancients' knowledge would seem to have been extraterrestrial in origin!

Studying the Maya, Hancock was amazed by the "computer-like circuitry" of their calendar and extraordinary precision of the calculated length planet orbits; it keeps track of eclipses, etc. Hancock proposed that the calendar was a bequest from a technologically advanced civilization of prehistory. He also thought that the image of Lord Pakal on his sarcophagus, with its "side panels, rivets, tubes and other gadgets", suggested a "technological device. Believing he had found the secret purpose of the Maya, Argüelles saw their wizard-king as representatives or avatars of galactic civilization that were post-technological".

For von Daniken, Lord Pakal was clearly an "ancient astronaut", operating the controls of some futuristic craft: *"This strange being wears a helmet from which twin tubes run backwards. In front of his nose is an oxygen apparatus. The figure is manipulating some kind of controls with both hands"*. (Daniel Pinchbeck, 2012 The return of Quetzalcoatl, 2006)

This forces us to radically reassess our attitude to the surviving works of antiquity, as they probably contain priceless information about the world around us, humanity, the true history of Earth and our astonishing ancestors.

When I read this sentence, tears start running from my eyes…. I was deeply touched…. Yes, here was the answer to my whole life's puzzles about my thousand unexplained dreams, visions and hypnosis sessions! All of this is part of the history of our planet and this is part of my past lives. Well what kind of expression will be on the author's face when I will tell him that his article made me cry? I guess he will be surprised.

"We now have a basic idea of the "source" of knowledge and can move on to the next stage: considering the reasons for the construction of the pyramids. In order to understand the interests of the ancients and the role that the pyramids played in attaining those interests, you will need to do what no one before you has done: form a basic conception about the fate of our civilization. This will not be easy, but do not look for easy paths on the way to truth… Let us turn the astronomical clock back 15,000 years. For the majority of Earth's population that knew of the existence of the Neferu, they remained mysterious with the aura of demigods."

Well, while I type this, I continue to cry right now – they're kind of happy tears. To have solved this mystery;

to know WHO I AM; not being afraid to share my dreams with people and talk about my ultra human abilities in my dreams and not to worry anymore that people would think that something is wrong with me or that I am just crazy (I am not) feels wonderful!. Here is the proof.

"Contact between the Neferu and Earthlings began long before the events described and was initiated by the Neferu themselves in the process of their exploration of the planets of the solar system. "The Neferu's level of development was so high that our contemporary science would simply be unable to accept it, although more than enough staggering facts have already been accumulated. In our opinion, the most mind-blowing physical evidence of the scientific and technical genius of the Neferu is the gigantic underground complex of meteorite and asteroid defenses constructed in what is now western Siberia."

Here is amazing example how this meteorite defense complex destroyed the Tunguska meteorite in 1908, the Sikhote-Alin meteorite in 1947, the Chulym bolide in 1984 and the Vitim meteorite on September 24, 2002.
"We earnestly recommend that you study the articles about this, published in NEXUS Magazine (vol. 11 no. 1, vol. 12 # 1–3). This asteroid defense system was the result of the Neferu's study of the—to a large extent tragic—history of the solar system. The fact is that on its journey through the galaxy, our planetary gyroscope passes cyclically—once in 33 million years, as it crosses the plane of the galaxy—through a meteor stream. Incidentally, 65 million years ago this stream killed off all the dinosaurs. More than once, this deadly rain has destroyed life-forms on Earth that were capable of developing intelligence.

"Preparation of Earthlings for more profound contact with the Neferu began with the formation of an elite capable of grasping the Neferu's ideology and conveying it to the people. To this end, the representatives of the Neferu made direct contact with the leaders of tribal alliances living in those parts of the globe in which the Neferu had particular interest. Argüelles proposed that the Tzolkin, their 260 - day ceremonial calendar, was the basis of Mayan esoteric technology, linking them to vast cosmic cycles and evolutionary patterns. The seemingly simple 13-by 20 matrix of the Tzolkin functioned as the basis of Mayan science and space travel, allowing them to receive and transmit information -as well as themselves-between star systems. He called Tzolkin the "Loom of Maya", and suggested they utilized in their science of divining harmony and creating resonant patterns – a science that was an art of being in the right place at the right time.

"Like galactic ants, the Maya and their civilization would be the synchronizers of momentary need-represented by planetary or solar intelligence-with universal purpose, fully conscious entry into the galactic community. Argüelles compared this mission with the goals of our present civilization: Who can say what the goals of our civilization are? Do these goals even have a relation to the planet, much less to the solar system? 'It was apparent simplicity and intricate subtleties of this Tzolkin, rather then "Encyclopedia Galactica", that the Maya had bequeathed to us to help us enter the community of galactic intelligence." (Daniel Pinchbeck, 2012 The Return of Quetzalcoatl, 2006)

"The next stage was the creation of a planet-wide communications system that provided the Neferu with extensive opportunities to stimulate the development of Earthlings' minds. To accomplish this highly complex task, a certain group of powerful Earthlings was given "instructions" on how to build structures in which they

133

would be able to hear the "voice of god" (the Neferu) and communicate with him."

(This explains why the pyramids in Egypt and Mexico have lots of similarities, simply because they receive this knowledge from the same source, the same "teacher". It also explains why, in Ancient Egypt and in Mexico, their Gods and Goddesses, elites, were wearing masks in ancient times, at the beginning of their development. Their Neferu "teacher" was under the masks. I had this feeling during my first hypnosis session when I was suddenly on the top of the Chichen Itza pyramid. The first thing I saw near me was an enormous Eagle head-mask, the size of which was much bigger than what a normal-size human would wear. It was a strange feeling that it was either a real half human and half eagle, or not a human at all, (under this mask).

"Through visits to the "house of god" (pyramid) on the days appointed by "the gods", the chosen ones would receive knowledge "of divine origin". Using this knowledge, they would be able to improve their health, acquire exceptional abilities, "listen to the universe" and see places elsewhere on Earth and beyond. In brief, the priests understood that the "gods" had chosen them for a great mission and that every step, every new achievement, would bring them closer to "the gods" and the "supernatural" qualities that "the gods" possessed."

Let's see this "supernatural" ability, which I had as a Priest from Neferu; let's go back to the dreams: Dream # 13 – The Upper Kingdom, October 24, 1993, where I fought with some terrible, black, big and hairy creature.

I have to fight. Then something surprising started to happen. I was looking at everything as if from some other, second sight. Suddenly there was two of me. Everything ended up very quickly – looking from the outside – incredibly simply and easily. The other me who was fighting did this – she was standing away at about two to three meters and then the beast lunged in my direction – at that same moment, that same second, an air stream appeared in front of him, very thin, it captured him then lunged and turned in the right direction. In front of him, there was something invisible, similar to a veil with gold threads, fibers, but incredibly taut and strong, like laser rays, twisted. There was a breath inside the veil, or something like a stream of air, invisible. This was in the air in front of him right at the moment he lunged at me with his armor. He hit the veil around him. His body was pulled into the threads, bending around and twisting to escape. It turned up, he hit, cut himself. Meanwhile I did nothing. I just stayed there and watched from the side. Yet I knew that I had created this air-wall with threads in front of him. And I noticed that the sickle, that had stricken him and was in his hands, looked actually like a laser disc, but larger, and incredibly thin and sharp.

And in the same dream I was in contact with the Neferu and I saw what their "airplane" looked like. I mention it before, but I read this article when I finished writing the book, so now I know who this THING is and where Kukulcan comes from, he belongs to the Neferu civilization.

I brought my creatures to this THING. Then something crawled out to meet me. It said to me, "I will save yours, the little ones." And it began to unwind, unroll, as if it was crawling out of an invisible crack in the wall. There was an opening and it crawled out – I didn't see the inside of the place. It was growing in size – expanding, and became as big as a Hercules plane. From the tail a huge crack opened across its body leading my creatures inside it. Its head was flat, like a leaf.

Let's continue with the article and find out why pyramids were built?

Tremendous prospects opened up before human beings, the significance of which exceeded any efforts required for their accomplishment. And they began working with a will. People started building pyramids in various parts of the world according to the plans and instructions given by "the gods". The unprecedented efforts of the Earthlings and, importantly, the Earthlings' own hands, created a complex that embraced the whole Earth in a spiral running from south to north. The complex of structures included pyramids, steles, dolmens, hills and mountaintops that were given a pyramidal shape. All the elements of the complex were erected on specially selected elevated features connected with energetically active geological faults that, in the Egyptian religious tradition, were known as "the Sacred Hills of the First Time". In all, 64 of these were chosen.

The distance between pyramids belonging to the complex was 5,000 kilometers. The dolmens—which (like the chambers of the pyramids) acted as resonators, amplifying particular energy flows—were placed directly on these faults, their openings facing a distant object belonging to the complex, forming an energy-carrying circuit. The pyramids, meanwhile, were constructed with a strict north-south orientation to their sides.

Dream # 23
Meeting Myself From The Future, October 30, 1987

I promised in The Priest book to tell you about this meeting. I was in Caracole, which is located in an area not far from the Caspian Sea at the border with Iran. Lots of pomegranates there! Beautiful! This area has the name of a unique piece of land named "Moon

Mountains", and listed in the book under "Wonders of the World".

Moon Mountains, Julia on the left

People are always afraid of the unknown and of things they don't understand.... There is nothing to be afraid of in this dream. It is just another dream.

****

I was inside some kind of capsule, in a transportation vehicle.

There is only one row of armchairs inside – two people in each section. In the hallway, there was an amazing child, maybe 130 cm high, standing in front of me. He looked straight at me. In order to see him better, I bent my knees and started peering into his face. He was something extremely beautiful, which I never saw in my life. I told him that I was a scientist and that I wanted to see him better, to study him.

Kukulcan

He told me that he knew everything about me, and he knew that I was a scientist, and he agreed. Next he told me that he was *me*, myself from another time! And that today, he wished to show me everything. He also told me that I could ask as much as I wanted. I was a guest this time, in their capsule and in their space. We communicated with each other without words, telepathically. I don't know what gender this adorable creature was.

He had a small child's face, a very small nose and mouth, and I guess he never used them. I think he never ate or took a breath. He had big elongated eyes and right next to the eyes, there was the edge of his helmet. Everything above that, from the forehead upwards, appeared large, disproportionate when compared to the small size of his face. There was a white glowing "halo" around his face, from ear-level. When I looked at it more closely, and observed the details, it was like a foggy smoke, light-ash and turquoise in color, like a colloid. You could almost see through it…. His face was of a darker color, the helmet was lighter and the "halo" was of a much lighter color yet.

Because of this, his head gave the impression that it was made of two layers. This child's face had a golden olive color. His cheeks were tinted in a coffee-olive-lilac color. He had emerald green eyes. Above the eyes, on the edge of the helmet there was a blue, thin crystal. The light from the crystal dropped on the olive face which gave it this beautiful radiating color. The blue crystal consisted of tiny tubes that looked very sharp. They were like one crystal that made up lots of other crystals – such as what you find in a geode. They pointed up at a 30 degree angle from the edge – as sharp as a shaving blade.

In front of the helmet there was an oval shaped scale and plate – and two of the same on both sides. This helmet enclosed his ears – if he had any – completely. There were orange crystals on the neck and a bright orange neon dot on the front of his neck in the middle at shoulder level. On the edge of each shoulder there was bright blue neon color.

All together it looked like an icon found in the churches. His entire body was covered with clothing – the only bare skin was his face. His clothes were made of scales – the same as his helmet.

He invited me to sit. I saw a woman sitting farther down the row and the seat next to me was empty. I looked at her hands and saw a very unusual bracelet. As soon as I woke up, I drew the bracelet, the child and the capsule.

There were many fragments in that dream. At first, we all sat down and a person, like this child, sat at the back and communicated with all the people together at once, telepathically. Other people were children with elongated eyes, except for this woman next to me. It was like a brain storming session when questions were posed and everyone tried to find an answer. I loved that game and participated fully!

At one point, the child asked me to look through the window. I recognized the place! We were next to the Russian Defense Ministry, in Moscow! This is not far from Red Square and the Bolshoi Theater. We flew very low! I saw people walking on the street and cars! We turned near the restaurant "Praga", where I usually ordered special gourmet cakes, and continued moving above the street, which crosses Kalininsky prospect, and then moved straight ahead of us. I was inside the capsule for only a few minutes by then. I wondered how we could possibly have covered 3500 miles in a few minutes – from the border of Iran to that far north. They showed me their technology. I asked everything I wanted and I tested almost everything, except for a few things, which they didn't allow me to touch and asked that I watched instead. There was a fence, which separated me from that area. I could only watch what they were doing in that space. They went on talking without words directly to my mind.

Nothing there compares to anything that we have here. It is hard to describe, impossible to find the right words. I wasn't afraid of them, I studied them. When people are afraid, it blocks their mind and their brain functions. It can be even dangerous sometimes, because they cannot control themselves. Another fragment of this dream describes these unusual people, maybe 8 or 10 of them, who did something odd with a black oval cylinder.[15] They knew how to twist space with it – they showed me how, I loved it! I very much wanted to participate in everything they did!

At one point, they invited me to take a ride on a very fast, very cute, little train, on very narrow rails, where there was only space for two people to sit. I loved that ride. I felt great! But what was most interesting is that I saw myself operating this black cylinder and working with beautiful crystals, like those I had in the Atlantis dreams! The crystals were of all colors in Atlantis. I remember the time, in the capsule, when a blue colored crystal turned to purple, violet when I activated it! It worked the same as it did when I worked with my crystals in Atlantis.

---

[15] This cylinder was a mystery to me, and I had a personal interest in it. I saw it many times and used it in my other dreams. It has something to do with energy and space, and I still don't know exactly what its purpose is.

****

This complicated configuration around the child's face made me think that a computer was perhaps incorporated in that helmet, placed directly on his head. Perhaps it was a translation centre, a camera, radio, you name it, there seemed to be everything in there. Great idea! (See photo – *Julia's original transcription of Dream #23.*)

Next, he told me that *he was me, myself from another time!* Well..., was it from another past or future life?

For instance, this black cylindrical object goes back to Sumerian time.

I just found the figurine of their Goddess Inanna, dating back 4000-years. They described all of the objects that they found during the excavation in the city of Mari in 1934. In Inanna's hands there is an unusual, large, cylindrical object, besides which there are two horns (the main external attribute of deities). You can also see bibs and a special design on her helmet. On the back of the neck there is a strange object, in the form of a rectangular box, attached directly to the "helmet". In this image, there is a series of crisscrossing strips or belts, which is well visible. On the other image, Inanna is dressed in overalls and goggles. The group of archeologists led by U. Andre has found, in a temple of God Ashur, a bas-relief located on the wall on which the goddess, Ishtar, wearing some goggles, headphones and a number of other devices, is visible. Enlil, addressing Inanna, "These subjects' names collectively mean *"ME"*, and the goddess *'That which compresses in the hand seven 'ME'.*" It is worthy to note that the glasses or their adaptations are a frequent detail on Sumerian graphics.

Kukulcan

I even found an image of that black Sumerian cylinder on the internet; it is made from solid black rock (perhaps basalt) with writing on it.

After this dream, and for years, I had dreams about friendship with this scale-clothed, unusual bunch of people. I even have a name for three of them.

****

The woman, who was sitting near me in the capsule had a very rare, unusually shaped bracelet, I never saw something like this before. However, eight years after I had that dream, I visited a retired model and actress, in Canada. During my visit, Beverly started showing her photos. In one of the photos, I saw exactly the same bracelet on her wrist! I asked her where the bracelet was now. She said that it was in a safe deposit box and that she had not worn it in the last seven years! Apparently, after she bought it, she wore it only a few times during the autumn of 1987 – the same year as when I had that dream! She said that she was too old to wear such a bracelet now. It was too elegant and rich, so it attracted attention all the time. I have this bracelet in my hand now. I gave her a present, which she really liked and bought the bracelet from her.

It looks like this child knew the future. He knew that I would meet Beverly eight years later, that I would find the bracelet, and the bracelet will be prove that all of this is real. And that I will believe in many lives and he was in my dream – he was *me,* myself from the future. Or the past, maybe?

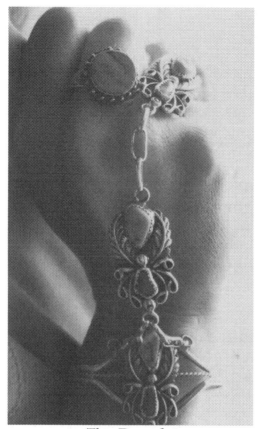

The Bracelet

It is good to know that we have extra time and that we have many lives – all kinds.

Since I saw that row of blue crystals near this child's eyes, all these years ago, I am using only blue mascara on my eyelashes. I also have green eyes like this child and I very much love everything made of silver or in silver color. I feel complete with it. [16]

---

[16] Maybe there is one more reason why I always use blue color mascara: (from a book on Egypt) "The eyes are painted and contoured around bright lapis-lazuli, under the white coating of the face – they are transparent. This impression of him may be

***

In order to be safe and not to lose yourself in that kind of dream, it is necessary to remember yourself at each moment, again and again, and again. Look around you, talk to all these Spirits and remember yourself, always return with your mind in time and space, fixing your position in your brain: "I am here; I am this little black point right now."

It is like a little fragment from your dream. It also helps to "save" the memory of your dreams. Your dreams are giving information to your brain portion by portion; you need to store the pieces in your memory like the files in your computer. This is how I remember most little details.

Dream # 24
You Are SvadiHatra! June 7, 1995

This dream occurred in the daytime. Around 3:00 p.m. a little man, 2.5" tall, was dancing and talking to me very fast; he was in a happy and funny mood!

"Did you call channel 5? You just call them, tell them about yourself, who you are!

"You are Svadihatra from the Galaxy Kvazi IN. This is how we call you. You always like to start flying with your crazy high speed from this long tube, in the "bee" house."

---

horrifying to the common people. Maybe this is the way how pharaohs colored there face to look like their Atlanteans teachers, Sumerians or even people from the future?" Remember Tutankhamen golden mask with blue line around the eyes and blue eyebrow?

He continued talking very, very fast... all kinds of things came out of his mouth. He poured information out, like a robot would read it to me, in a monotone voice – no inflexion in his speech, not as we usually talk – no pause either. Just round words, like beads rolling out of his mouth in a stable voice, with no emotions.

It was the same kind of dream with lots of information coming to me at high speed, such as in Dream # 7 – Arabian and American Mountains – 2 pyramids: Egypt and Mexico, October 25, 1990 (see, "The Re-birth of an Atlantean Queen", by Julia SvadiHatra).

His voice was talking to me very quickly – humans cannot talk that fast – it was saying different things, which I could not memorize. The views were replacing each other, the voice followed with information – very even; all phrases were similar, spoken like a robot. The letters were like little beads tumbling down through my ears at incredible speed.

Channel 5 in Vancouver is where you find TV programs about inventions, science, UFO, extraterrestrials and so on.

I have only a short version of this dream; I don't know where the full version is. Maybe I will find it one day. It was a month before I gave birth to my baby. I remember more but I don't want to add anything now. All of my dreams were transcribed directly from their original version on paper, which was written right after I woke up.

Julia's original transcription of Dream #23

The funny part is that he said that I was from the Galaxy Kvazi IN. It sounded the same as when we say, "She is from the Western Inn or Holiday Inn...."

So my name is *Svadihatra* when I fly in my dreams, at crazy speed across the Universe, while I visit galaxies, planets and stars, wearing this narrow helmet. Well, I don't take a passport with me into my dreams, but at least now, I know that I have some identity in the Universe....

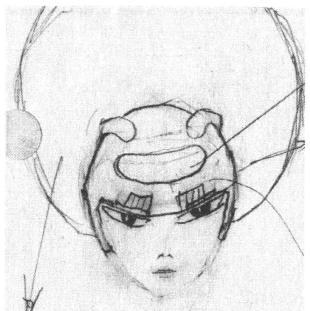

Svadihatra

I decided to check if there was any meaning behind the name. It meant nothing together, but the two words: **Svadi** **and** **Hatra** separately support WHO I AM amazingly well!

Svadi

From Wikipedia, the free encyclopedia,
http://en.wikipedia.org/wiki/Svadi
Giant Svadi from Dovre Mountain live in the north.... Sea king, who is called Svadi.

Yes, this is right to the point. I saw many times, in my dreams, giant people and I saw myself the same size as well.

Amazingly also, in Svadi, all letters that I have in my present last name are the same!

By the way I just visited Istanbul and I was in the Topkapi Palace. This palace was the Imperial residence

147

of Ottoman sultans for almost 400 years. I saw an enormous size sultan's outfit. I asked one of the guides in that room, why did the sultan have such big kaftans and pants, was he a huge size man, a giant? She replied that, yes, it was possible. This is it? Possible? Just see this photo!

The woman in front of the display could easily fit entirely into the Kaftan's shirt

Giant size kaftan belongs to sultan (IV.) Murad'a Afteditir (1623-1640)

It is prohibited to take photos in that room, so I could only take a photo of the kaftans, because the display cabinet with the pants was in the middle of the room, where the museum guides were standing most of the time. The sultan's pants were maybe 180 to 190 cm long, so this sultan should have been at least four meters tall!!

Kaftan

This is no "trick photography" – it seems as if I am "slipping" into the kaftan.

Maybe it was my Spirit Guide who wanted to tell me that this kaftan belonged to me before?

Maybe I was that sultan, Svadi in one of my past lives – Giant, who lived in this area?

Hatra

From Wikipedia, the free encyclopedia,
http://en.wikipedia.org/wiki/Hatra

Hatra (Arabic: al- al-   a   r) is an ancient ruined city in the Iraq.

The city had temples to Nergal (Sumerian and Akkadian), Hermes (Greek), Atargatis (Syro-Aramaean), Allat and Shamiyyah (Arabian) and Shamash (the Mesopotamian sun god).[2]

Each shrine was named after a single god, and with the development of the wide ranging Sumerian civilization these gods became part of a Pantheon or single family of divinities, known as the Annunaki (Anu = Heaven, Na = And, Ki = Earth).

149

Kukulcan

With the growth in size and importance of the temples, so the temple functionaries (priests = Sumerian sanga) grew in importance in their communities, and a hierarchy developed led by the En, or chief priest. Thus the chief priest of the God of Air (Lil) at the E-kur temple at the city of Nippur became "Enlil", and gods became more and more anthropomorphic.

Hatra is one of the ten Legendary Lost Cities of Tayyab. Hatra is a UNESCO World Heritage Site.

As you read my dreams through this book and hypnosis sessions, you see that I am the size of a normal human being, to 3 to 4 meters, to the size of a giant of about 8 meters and even much, much bigger – of an enormous size, maybe 50 meters or bigger, as a huge God looking down at me from the sky. These are things that my dreams repeated many times and there are hundreds of dreams already like these. The more I study my dreams, the more I understand that all of this was more than real a long time ago on Earth. The same is the case with that Atlantean woman and her ultra modern environment with most advance technology, which allowed her to travel in space at extremely high speed. Scientists found these devices and even a small computer, the size of a calculator, on the ocean floor in the drowned Atlantis. I continue to study the history of our Earth these days to find an answer to the question, "WHO AM I?"

I guess that all of the people who live on Earth have a long chain of lives going back to ancient times. I am lucky that I have the ability to remember lots of things in my dreams, right down to the smallest details. Also, deep hypnosis sessions help in making the pictures clearer.

So it seems that my Spirit come to this ancient part of Iran, Iraq and Turkey, as a Neferu and Nephilim (please see below, why), next was born as a Sumerian Priest, maybe giant Svadi in Turkey, later in Atlantis as a woman of importance, who was queen with priest responsibility at the same time and after in Mexico as a Priest as well. Somewhere in between, as an Egyptian royal girl with the crown and many more, which I did not check yet. I have dreamed about living in Holland or Belgium around the 16th century. I continue to study myself, my dreams and history of our blue planet. In the last two I was Amelia and now Julia. As you see it is a line of PRIESTS here. In all this past lives I was PRIEST or PRIESTESS. I find why when I study article of the Dr. Valery Uvarov.

I mentioned Neferu or Nephilim, because I had hundreds of dreams where I am of an enormous size and, yes, with goddess-like abilities such as it is described in HIDDEN TWIN AND THE BIRTH OF CIVILIZATION by Dr Valery Uvarov, Nexus magazine, #15 Vol.5)

About Nephilim:

Here is an excerpt about the statue of Nephilim in Afghanistan:

The city of Bamian is located in Afghanistan, between Kabul and Bal. Near this city there are five colossal statues of people from five previous races. The biggest one is a 52-meter man from the first Ephemera race. The sculpture is wrapped in a blanket that may indicate or symbolize its once fragile form. The second is 36 meters tall, the third is 18 meters tall and only the last two are the size of normal human beings.

Kukulcan

Afghanistan, city of Bamian colossal statue of giant from previous race

By the way, 52 meters is the size of a 12- or 14-storey building, depending on ceiling heights. It is interesting that in my dreams I saw myself sometimes enormously tall, looking down from the sky, onto my second little self – two of me at once.

I think that the big people in my dreams – ATHARVAN, October 13, 1989; ZARATUSTRA IN WATER, September 6, 1993 – belong to Nephilim. They are both with Persian and alien almond-shaped eyes.

Also Sumerian Goddesses Nephilim had symbols and things in their hands, outfits, which my "friends" and I were using in my dreams, when I traveled through Space. One of the drawing description of the Sumerian

Goddess Inanne show her that she with a black cylinder, helmet, overalls, goggles and even headphones. But I don't remember that I use or have any of this attributes while I was Atlantean woman living in the Earth as a fragile very light spirit human-angel kind of person, which I guess arrive from the Heaven.

Now, when the book is finished I see Dream # 19 Luminous Bodies of Plants, January 8, 1992 in a different light:

"You opened a book and started reading – a prologue. You were reading aloud with my voice. At the same time, the other me, was observing the scene from outside. I interrupted your reading. I knew what was written there, right away, although I heard it for the first time.

"In this book, the knowledge comes to the surface, which was unknown to people until then. This book was a revelation. People did not even suspect it – it opened up, revealing itself like an old secret, a treasure, as if someone dug it out of the earth. A very rare animal, a diamond animal was buried there thousands and thousands of years ago. I interrupted myself and started dictating the already specific things from this book (you had only the introduction). You started to write down what I was saying immediately."

It is interesting that in 1988 I was introduced to Nina, a psychic. As soon as she looked at me she told me, "I see you sitting in front of an enormous book and you are reading it." Two years later, I met the opera singer, Slava, who also has physic ability – the vibration of his voice is healing people. Suddenly he told me that he sees me as a Priest on the steps of big pyramid...

Kukulcan

I am sure that if scientists would make a list of questions about ancient civilizations like Sumerians, Atlantis, Ancient Egypt and Mexico, and started asking me these questions during some deep hypnosis sessions, I would shift in to this "diamond animal", which would be a rare and unique source for people to receive treasure from many Ancient civilizations: their deep secrets, knowledge about super human possibilities, ultra advanced technology and the deep, wise connections that exist between people and nature.

From my experience during the hypnosis sessions, what happens each time is that I turn instantly into this ancient person and respond to any question without thinking. Words come out automatically, directly from that person with his or her voice; the muscles on the face move in a different way and I, Julia, can't do anything about it. I am in a position of a silent witness to all of this. The first time it happened, I was in deep shock; afterwards I started getting used to it. After my first hypnoses session I said, "It was overwhelming and I didn't have any control over what was going on. I never had experienced something like this in my entire life..."

So, it was right for me to choose the pen-name *SvadiHatra* as the author of this book and another.

Now, following my example, perhaps you can imagine WHO YOU ARE: Your own Spirit can also have a chain of many re-born lives, back to very ancient times and you may have had deep experiences at all levels, all kinds of people have lived and re-lived on this planet.

So did you remember what is most important to remember for you and me and every one of us here on Earth?

"I am myself, not more than somebody else and not less then somebody else," and after say your own name.

I advise you to make this adjustment for yourself and you will be just fine, totally okay.
Alfons Ven, http://www.alfonsven.org/. See also the book, "The Re-birth of an Atlantean Queen"

The Universe is full of all kinds of Spirits, Angels, Creatures, Entities, good and bad, by the way, so be careful!

And YES, God and Goddesses exist there as well.

People from the past and the future are just a small part of it and most importantly they are actually who we are, ourselves from the future, for example. Nothing more.

Yes, they have advanced technology, so what? It is not the most important thing, actually. Try to imagine yourself living all your life in an airplane? Not much fun, is it? As for me, I prefer to visit nature, plants. *They* visit us here to learn from people much more important things: which only humans can create, emotions which they don't have, feelings, smiles, laughter, love, possibility to create poems, songs, music and those heavenly beautiful rays of God's creative energy from our eyes.
For some important reason, you and I were born humans.

Start studying yourself and ask; "Where are you going in this life?"

WHO ARE YOU?

Conclusion:

I think the Spirit body looks like a 3-D hologram, with some sort of crystal-like appearance. For some reason, I always see my Spirit as a perfect, strong crystal, as perfect as a diamond.

Our body is covered with an energy field, which is actually a matrix, a plan of the body structure. Inside our body there are over a million biochemical changes occurring every second. Our body is in constant changes. This plan around the body controls its functions and re-builds everything according to that plan. Maybe this energy field structure is responsible for our thinking process and consciousness. The thinking brain can only exist on biochemical or at the molecular and atom levels, where the possibility of "containers" for the consciousness on the level of elemental particles and their fields may exist. The Biofield is an ideal environment for *fluctuation*, which are holograms. It is possible to say that the biofield is actually a multi-component hologram. This way all of the person's life experiences – all his words, thoughts, words he ever said or someone said to him, what he saw, what he felt, all of his emotions – everything is preserved in that biofield in the form of holograms. These sets of holograms together form a kind of crystal, which we could name Soul or Spirit. (You will find more about our Spirit's characteristics at the end of the book, The Rebirth of an Atlantean Queen, in Scientific Interpretations section – Discovery of biofield)

In addition, I am sure the crystals' structure of the Spirit is the best to collect and save information from one lifetime to the next. The same as with any kind of information, to preserve it on the real crystals is much better than using something like CDs, DVDs or paper.

I am thinking now that when people travel through the Universe in their dreams, what we call here, an "astral body" is actually this crystal made from sets of many hologram components. It is interesting that the body of the person, who left with visitors from another planet to see their world, did not exist in time and space. Maybe it is transformed into the field structure, because this is the only way of entering the world of the field forms.

In the dream below, I tried to describe the crystallization process of my body as a preparation for space travel.

Dream # 41. A Gray Dumb-Bell in the Head, September 4, 1991 (see, "The Re-birth of an Atlantean Queen", by Julia SvadiHatra).
I had not fallen asleep deeply yet, I still remember myself, when some substance of gray color entered my head from both sides and started to crystallize inside it. It was not a pipe, the whole thing was filled in, crystallized all at once, and it was fitting very well...

However, when a person returns to our reality, to our world, that "plan structure around the body" shows amazing capabilities for analyzing and collecting components and for regeneration; returning these components into their previous structure, not only at the body level, but also at the level of consciousness and emotions.

Maybe while we are here on Earth, in the form of physical bodies, we are collecting some experiences into this energy field, crystal structure, named Soul or Spirit. After the biological body dies, we fly toward the Universe Consciousness with all of these new qualities that we accumulated during our life as a human in the physical, materialistic world, where the field-form from Space just cannot develop at all.

Table of Common Characteristics

Common things in life; characters, habits, looks, interests, activities in the lives of the four people, who lived from 70 years, to 2 thousand and 10 thousand years apart from each other.

CHARACTERISTICS	AMELIA EARHART	JULIA SVADI HATRA	MAYA PRIEST	QUEEN OF ATLANTIS
Healing & Medicine	Yes	Yes	Yes	Yes
Basketball	Yes	Yes	Yes	No
Biology, agriculture, herbal plants	Yes	Yes	Yes	Possible
Math	Yes	Yes	Yes	Yes
Maps; land & sky	Yes	Yes	Yes	Possible
Airplanes, aviation, travel in space	Yes	Yes	Yes	Yes
Black hairy creatures *"Jabberwocky"*	Yes	Yes	Yes	
Love stars, addiction to the sky	Yes	Yes	Yes	Yes
Can't drink tea, coffee	Yes	Yes		
Tomato Juice	Yes	Yes		
Lougheed as an airplane & nurse's last name	Yes	Yes		
Hart and Hatra	Yes	Yes		
Flower named Amelia Jasmine Rose Lily	Yes	Yes		Possible
Twin trees with couples' names	Yes	Yes		
Leadership	Yes	Yes	Yes	Yes
High responsibility	Yes	Yes	Yes	Yes
Strength of character, brave nature	Yes	Yes	Yes	Yes
Responsible for the well-being of her people, society community	Yes	Yes	Yes	Yes
Hunting	Yes	Yes	Yes	
Ghost, Atchison "Most Ghostly Town in USA"	Yes	Yes	Yes	

CHARACTERISTICS	AMELIA EARHART	JULIA SVADI HATRA	MAYA PRIEST	QUEEN OF ATLANTIS
Curse	Yes	Yes	Yes	
Importance of numbers	Yes	Yes	Yes	Yes
Persistence and perseverance	Yes	Yes	Yes	Yes
Lots of followers, pioneers	Yes	Yes	Yes	Yes
Studying, sciences	Yes	Yes	Yes	Yes
Open new freedom and new possibilities	Yes	Yes		
Drowning	Yes	Yes	Unknown	Possible
Problems with own children	Yes	Yes	Yes	Yes
Worker in charge of children, teaching	Yes	Yes	Yes	
Big "ego"	Yes	No	Yes	No
Adoring Asia – Japan, China	Yes	Yes	Unknown	Yes
Fine Arts	Yes	Yes	Yes	Yes
Physics, studies the sounds of the rocks, energy, transportation	Yes	Yes	Yes	Yes
Music, sounds	Yes	Yes	Yes	Unknown
Poetry	Yes	Yes	Unknown	
Chemistry	Yes	Yes	Possible	
Zoology	Yes	Yes	Possible	
Pacifist	Yes	Yes	Unknown	Yes
Supreme intelligence	Yes	Yes	Yes	Yes
Same facial features	Yes	Yes	No	Yes
Deeply spiritual	Yes	Yes	Yes	Yes
Creativity	Yes	Yes	Yes	Yes
True love	Yes	Yes	Possible	Yes
Thick hair	Yes	Yes	Yes	Yes
Extensive travel	Yes	Yes	Possible	Possible
Martial Arts, tomboy	Yes	Yes	Yes	NO
Fear of "lost for ever"	Yes	Yes		
Younger sister	Yes	Yes		
Angry black dog	Yes	Yes		
Someone named Mary	Yes	Yes		

Kukulcan

CHARACTERISTICS	AMELIA EARHART	JULIA SVADI HATRA	MAYA PRIEST	QUEEN OF ATLANTIS
Girlfriends named Laura in school	Yes	Yes		
"Extreme" people in extreme situations	Yes	Yes	Yes	Yes
Pilot shirt, similar clothing	Yes	Yes		
Astrology	Unknown	Yes	Yes	Yes
Jaguar skin, or print clothes		Yes	Yes	
Tortoise (turtle)		Yes	Yes	
White jaguar		Yes	Yes	
Connection with the Goddess, meeting with God		Yes	Yes	Yes
Word Caracol		Yes	Yes	
Word *Equinox* talking in ancient Maya		Yes	Yes	
Priesthood, priest's connection		Yes	Yes	Yes
Intuition, predictions	Yes	Yes	Yes	Yes
Masks		Yes	Yes	
Sacrifices		Yes	Yes	
Aztec God Xochipilli		Yes	Yes	
Addiction to crystals, growing crystals, diamonds, museums, factories		Yes	Yes	Yes
Playing the same "Rock from the past"		Yes	Yes	
Laser, X-ray technology, studied seeds		Yes	Yes	Yes
Book opening up like an accordion, website moving bar, business plan		Yes	Yes	
Spirit support		Yes	Yes	
Big, tall people		Yes	Yes	Yes
Materialization, teleportation, moving objects		Yes		Yes

I recognize now that I am lucky in life, because I had the rare possibility to see the chain of my past lives, the echoes from my past, and make adjustments to my future, spiritual development.

These four people had the same Spirit, which was transferred from the life of one person to the next and to the next. Skills, habits, experience, and knowledge accumulated in the Spirit holographic crystal are transferred with the Spirit to the next newborn person as an inheritance from all of his past lives. This is the chain of lives of people who carried the same Spirit. The Spirit of the people is ETERNAL.

The Smartest People In The World Are Trying To Tell You Something

There are probably other parallel universes in our living room

"There are vibrations of different universes right here, right now. We're just not in tune with them. There are probably other parallel universes in our living room—this is modern physics. This is the modern interpretation of quantum theory, that many worlds represent reality."

Dr. Michio Kaku, Theoretical Physicist, Professor and Bestselling Author

...There are an infinite number of parallel realities coexisting with us in the same room

"There are hundreds of different radio waves being broadcast all around you from distant stations. At any given instant, your office or car or living room is full of these radio waves. However if you turn on a radio, you can listen to only one frequency at a time; these other frequencies are not in phase with each other. Each station has a different frequency, a different energy. As a result, your radio can only be turned to one broadcast at a time. Likewise, in our universe we are *tuned into the frequency that corresponds to physical reality. But there are an infinite number of parallel realities coexisting with us in the same room, although we cannot tune into them."

Professor Steven Weinberg, Nobel Prize in Physics (1979)

"In infinite space, even the most unlikely events must take place somewhere. People with the same appearance, name and memories as you, who play out every possible permutation of your life choices."

Professor Max Tegmark, Dept. of Physics, MIT

We are facing a revolution in our thinking about the physical universe

"Today, probably more than in any other day, we are facing a revolution in our thinking about the physical universe—the stuff that you and I are made of. This revolution, brought to a head by the discoveries of the new physics, including relativity and quantum mechanics, appears to reach well beyond our preconceived vision, based as it was on the concept of concrete solid reality."

Dr Fred Alan Wolf, Author and Physicist

If a universe can be imagined, it exists.

Professor M.R. Franks, Member, Royal Astronomical Society of Canada

An ensemble of other different universes is necessary for the existence of our universe.

Professor John D. Barrow, Dept. of Applied Mathematics and Theoretical Physics, Cambridge University

We all exist in multiple universes...

"...but we only carry our own perception of our universe. We walk in our own bubble of reality without time or space and create our own universe."

Gerald O'Donnell, Leading Expert in the Military Science of Remote Viewing

I could go on and on here, because there's countless other intellectuals that have made discoveries in the possibility of alternate universes, including the world-famous Professor Stephen Hawking, Professor Alan Guth, and even Albert Einstein himself.

If you need more proof, just try Googling scientific theories like String Theory and M-Theory, or watch the film 'What The Bleep'. But for now, check out this unbelievable story...

Burt Goldman *http://www.quantumjumping.com/*

Sources:

João's behaviour. (The Miracle Man: The Life Story of João de Deus, by Robert Pellegrino-Ostrich. Extracted from his book Published in 1997, ©1997/1998 All Rights Reserved).
MONTERREY, Mexico, Sept 24 (Reuters Life!) -
Maya Gods and Goddesses, CRYSTALINKS.
(Can Humpty Dumpty be put back together again? Gene D. Matlock © Copyright 2005).
Rudyard Kipling, Rikki-Tikki-Tavi
http://www.crystalinks.com/
http://www.crystalinks.com/quetzalcoatl.html
http://www.crystalinks.com/sumergods.html
http://africa.reuters.com/wire/news/usnN24278139.html
http://en.wikipedia.org/wiki/Svadi
http://en.wikipedia.org/wiki/Hatra
Valery Uvarov, *Earth's Hidden Twin and the Birth of Civilization* (Nexus magazine, #15 Vol.5)
Akaija is a unique healing device and jewelry made by Akaija & Art www.akaija.com
http://www.akaija.com/info/UK/UK06_3D.shtml
http://www.akaija.com/info/UK/UK05_gallery.shtml
Russian Astronaut drawing
http://www.veoh.com/videos/v554944aTQShtQA?g=cccp&rank=13&order=ca
A. Vasiliev, "Miracles and Adventures", newspaper, *Secret Doctrina*, #13, July 2007
http://www.quantumjumping.com/ Burt Goldman

Testimonials

Reading your book but I am crying so much reading I can hardly read it. Your book resonates so much with me, so much emotions it brings up. You put your heart in this book to touch the hearts of the readers.
Buryl Payne.

I really do think from what I wrote that you are an amazing woman, someone that comes along once in a life time. You are a real live Goddess! Most priceless alive human on the planet at our time. I really mean it is Incredible! Your outlook on life, philosophy and spiritual beliefs are outstanding and intriguing. Your dreams are very smart, unusual, bright and full of dynamic. It attracts like a magnet to read your wise book. Intelligence far beyond normal. What is your IQ?
Henry D.

Best book to take to the banker!
It will never be boring to read it over and over again for many years!
Your book like a jewelry box for me, which if you would open it; you would be astonished seeing the flush of rare, magic multicolored things inside it. You are AVATAR who opened this rare knowledge to all of us.
hurrican888

I dreamed about you last night and the overall theme was: connected by the light and flying through space.... it made me very happy, I have had many past lives, also in Atlantis, Egypt etc., so no doubt we know each other.
Marianne Notschaele-den Boer www.vorigelevens.nl

Wow! I guess I discovered real treasure here!
silvercrystall

Kukulcan

That is so wonderful, and you should be so very proud of yourself. Just think of the impact that you can have on the lives of others through your book...opening up their minds, their spirituality, their soul, and their current lives!!!!!!"
Christopher M.

Afraid to die? Just read front page of that website!
http://www.ameliareborn.com/
and you will never afraid again! Never! Can't wait to read whole book... Amazing!
Miracleforest

Where to order the book:

For any information, please visit the website:
http://www.ameliareborn.com/
www.ameliareborn.com

Or contact me at:

contact@ameliareborn.com

YOU TUBE
amelia reborn

2012MayaPriest

To buy this or any of Julia SvadiHatra's five books on line, please visit Amazon.com, BarnesandNobles.com, Borders.com or ChapterIndigo.com and write the title of your choice in the "search window".

Kukulcan

Acknowledgements

Thanks to Mr. Jorge Esma Bazan, Director of Patronato Culture, State of Yucatan, Mexico and to his great team for their effort in keeping the architectural complex of Chichen Itza and other historical monuments in Yucatan in excellent, perfect condition. Their highly organized planning and the maintenance of international levels of standards provide the tourists with the wonderful opportunity to enjoy such important events as the "Equinox in Chichen Itza".

Grateful thanks to Wilma Herrada Dodero, who navigated me with good advices, help and support while I was in Yucatan, Mexico.

To dear Alfons Ven who taught me to ask myself: "Who am I?" His genius gave me the unique possibility to return my self and others to our own selves by using his "miracle pills", changing our lives forever. It helped me in opening the doors to a waterfall of my own enormous amount of energy and in staying in great, dynamic health, optimistic and happy.

Special, deeply felt thanks to the wise, Diana Cherry, who, over the last 60 years, has helped thousands of people getting rid of the heavy burden of their past and find out *who* they really were through studying their Spirit Journey and seeing their lives under a new light.

Special thanks to Roxane Christ, my editor, who encouraged and supported me during the writing of this book. With her thorough knowledge of the language, she helped me, and many other authors, bring our books to life and make them available to readers. She put her full attention and kind heart into my book, and it was a great pleasure working with her.

I express special thanks to my ex-husband, Tim. I shall acknowledge the massive efforts of laboriously collecting and systematizing the dreams, which are used in this book, as well as for the production of the beautiful covers.

168

Thanks to Carlos Castaneda for the invention of new terminology, which helped me, and many other authors all over the world, to describe the Spirit world. Going through his books, his message became perfectly clear. I guess because of my past life experience as an ancient Maya Priest, I could read between the sentences what was impossible for him to describe or put into words.

Thanks to the wonderful Crystalinks Metaphysical and Science Website which provided with great image sources and information about Ancient Civilizations and helped me with my research.

Thank you to Valery Uvarov for the article *Earth's Hidden Twin and the Birth of Civilization.* His research helped to put the last pieces of the puzzle in the right places and solve a life long mystery for me, making it possible to see the complete picture of the history of civilization on our planet, as well as my past lives, which are now laid down in harmony.

Special thanks to brave Amelia Earhart who flew the World and became a legend. This enormous effort and her achievements were made available to me in a full and detailed account of her life. It helped me in comparing my life, the life of an Ancient Maya Priest with her life and proved that the Spirit of each person on Earth has many lives. I am deeply grateful for the gift she passed onto me, as a newborn person, who now carries the same Spirit: her experience and knowledge in biology, medicine, art, writing, and drawing, which she acquired and developed during her lifetime. I am thankful for her enormous strength and love for life and adventure. All of this priceless Spirit development is deeply appreciated by all other re-born people in these Spirits and those who will be reborn in future and continue to carry Spirit light through the chain of lives.

Thanks to the Ancient Maya Priest who gave me wisdom, knowledge about the other side of life: energy, auras, how to connect with Spirits, Gods and Goddesses. All of which were passed onto me in the form of an amazing friendship with plants, animals and echoing rocks; understanding their tender souls. I am also grateful to him for passing onto me his enormous strength, love and care for his people. He helped them survive through terrible droughts in Mexico

Kukulcan

and he was strong enough to sacrifice his own son for their wellbeing.

To my lifelong friend and companion in my dreams, the Holy Spirit, my Guide who lives somewhere in the Universe, on the Other Side and for giving me support, helping me travel in my dreams through the planet and our Universe. He is the one who was talking to me throughout the years, teaching me and educating me in my dreams and helping me connect with other Spirits, Gods and Goddesses. I give you prayerful thanks.

To some amazing High Power and to my extended family on the Other Side, who are my Guardian Angels, who care about me, and who help me navigate in this life to avoid danger, make the right decisions and warn me ahead of time by talking to me daily through the numbers' code, I give thanks.

Special thanks to GOD who blessed me and saved my life, and as a result, enabling me to write this book.

Read More...

In the book, "**THE PRIEST**" you will find details of Julia's SPIRIT JOURNEY from her life as an Ancient Mayan Priest of Chichen Itza. 2000 years old secrets revealed: how he performed ceremonies and rituals on top of the pyramid, the Spirit world, sacrifices, symbols and the life of the ancient Maya people in Chichen Itza – a Message from them to the present-day civilization passed on to us. Meeting with God and angels, contacts with ancient Goddesses, Persian Goddesses, new Atharvan images, Zarathustra, ghosts, visiting a real Buddhist temple ... are all in Ancient Priest of Chichen Itza reincarnated by Julia SvadiHatra.

In the book, "**WHO IS CHAK MOL?**" you will find who the Ancient Priest meets in Chichen Itza! Guess who it was? A Mexican hero, Chak Mol! You will find out who he was; where he came from before arriving in Mexico and Chichen Itza and even who his mother was! He was a giant Atlantean man! You will find out where he lived and where he played in Chichen Itza.

In the book, "**AMELIA REBORN?**" Amelia is talking to us. Astonishing secrets are revealed. Was Amelia meant to die according to some "secret plan"? Through the author's past life experience, Amelia is able to describe the last minutes before her death, how she enters Heaven. Why was she lost? Why is it impossibly difficult to find her? Is it a curse by ancient Egyptian or Mexican spirits on those who are "playing games" around Amelia's disappearance?

What is common between Amelia and the Ancient Priest of Chichen Itza?

Kukulcan

In this book you will also find details of Amelia's SPIRIT JOURNEY from her life in Ancient Egypt. Did Amelia belong to a royal family of Ancient Egypt or was she a Priestess there? A unique Egypt's ancient initiation ceremony of a Goddess, meeting with Egyptian Goddesses and magic of the Holy Spirit of Bast, the Royal Cat Goddess, intriguing Anubis, communication with an Ancient Priest & Pharaoh, swimming in the efir oils, present to the Great Cheops pyramid, ancient ritual inside the tomb, talking to mummies, GIANT Pharaohs... are all in this truly Mysterious Magic Egypt.

In the book, **"THE REBIRTH OF AN ATLANTEAN QUEEN"** you will find the complete story about the Spirit Journey of Amelia and all her other past lives as a Priest of Chichen Itza, an Atlantean Queen, Ancient Egyptian royal Priestess, Julia Svadihatra and even one future life. This big book contains all 4 books we just mentioned: Priest, Who is Chak Mol, Amelia Reborn, Kukulcan and an additional chapter: The Rebirth of an Atlantean Queen about life in Atlantis. Was Amelia an Atlantean Queen in her past life? Did she carry with her secrets of the crystal pyramid and how to re-ignite its energy? In this book Amelia's Spirit went back to her past life in Atlantis and her abilities began to emerge in this life time in a new re-born person!
Enjoy reading.

Exclusive editor of all 5 books:
Roxane Christ, www.1steditor.biz

Appendix

The sure way to evolve from now on into a better self!

Alfons Ven, an Engineer, turned healer out of necessity.

Alfons Ven devised a 28-day "Matrix Support Program" to evolve
from now on "into a better self".
Giving everybody a chance to live a healthy and *victorious* life.

THE MATRIX OF TWELVE ASPECTS

It all started with a vision. How plants overcame their fear to be
devoured, and were endowed with subtle invisible information to
overcome and control it.
That insight evolved further into Twelve Aspects. (See figure
below.)
Each Aspect covers specific regulating evolutionary patterns.
Alfons introduces these patterns onto pills giving readjusting
instructions to man, in order to

- Clarify and be at peace with the past.
- Get better attuned with the Invisible.
- Discover and live the real, original you.
- Live a safe and well-balanced existence.
- Realize what you imagine.
- Unlock your personality.
- Boost your awareness.
- Free your spirit.
- Restore your soul.
- Heal your body and mind
- Evolve from now on into better.
- Reap the fruits of progress and growth.

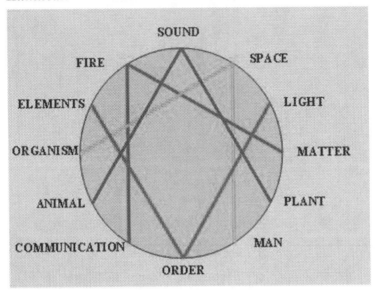

The conditions are simple:
- Just start with a "Matrix Support Program".
- Let it happen and rely on your *'automatic goal-striving, built-in regulating system'*.
- Respect your very best nature.
- Commit to good causes and realistic goals.
- Stay focused and grateful.
- Act swiftly when opportunity knocks.

The "Matrix Support Program" is inserted in a blister pack – easy to use. Over the 28-day program, a few little sugar pills are taken. It's that simple. The pills are inert. Meaning that no chemical substance has been added during their manufacturing. Therefore, there are no side effects, no possible overdose. Young and old – man and animal alike – can safely use them.
The patterns on the pills affect the *invisible* part of us and are not to be taken as a medicine in the literal or scientific sense.

Where to begin?

STEP-1
The Step-1-Program is equipped to deal with a wide range of problems – to clear up many hidden issues while readjusting your body as a whole. It's also an extensive grounding treatment. It assists in the constitutional upgrade and the rebalancing of the metabolism. It also facilitates the reintegration of the 'Twelve Aspects'. It has a deep restoring effect on the immune system.

STEP-2
If one feels that there are still some unresolved issues, it is recommended to state the issues in an e-mail. A personalized Step-2-Program can then be designed for your particular needs. This may be repeated to upgrade your functionality even more.

STEP-3
This Step is an invitation to progress and growth, to assist you further in the fine-tuning to the Twelve Aspects.

THE ALFONS VEN FOUNDATION
Has been helping people worldwide since 1996. Amazing testimonials of healing and changes of life for the better keep streaming in daily.
Whatever your issues are, whatever you tried before, the "Matrix Support Program" is always an asset.

Notes: Helpdesk: myriam@alfonsven.com or call: +31 30 233 3188
Website: www.alfonsven.com
Statement: The Alfons Ven Foundation is not affiliated with any *political, religious, esoteric, spiritual groups or organizations* whatsoever.